Living the Mystery

Monastic Markers on
the Christian Way

To the Oblates of Pluscarden Abbey
and of St Mary's, Petersham

Living the Mystery

Monastic Markers on the Christian Way

Dom Hugh Gilbert, OSB

GRACEWING

First published in 2008

Gracewing
2 Southern Avenue
Leominster
Herefordshire HR6 0QF

ISBN 978 0 85244 692 8

Typeset by Action Publishing Technology Ltd
Gloucester GL1 5SR

Contents

Part III: Bearing Fruit

Note

Scriptural references are taken from the RSV Bible, unless specified otherwise. Quotations from the psalms are from the Grail translation as used in the Divine Office, unless otherwise indicated.

Introduction

'How blessed, how marvellous are the gifts of God, my friends! Some of them, indeed, already lie within our comprehension – the life that knows no death, the shining splendour of righteousness, the truth that is frank and full, the faith that is perfect assurance, the holiness of chastity – but what of the things prepared for those who wait? Who but the Creator and Father of eternity, the Most Holy himself, knows the greatness and the beauty of these? Then let us strain every nerve to be found among those who wait in patience for Him, so that we too may earn a share of His promised gifts.'[1]

Such words, written around the year AD 96 by Pope Clement to the Christians of Corinth, express like many another passage from early Christian writers the sheer delight the first Christians experienced in the life – its goodness, truth and beauty – which they knew they had entered upon through faith and participation in the sacraments.

'And it is by that very way, dear friends, that we find our own salvation: namely Jesus Christ, the High Priest by whom our gifts are offered, and the Protector by whom our feebleness is aided. Through Him we can look up to the highest heaven and see, as in a glass, the peerless perfection of the face of God. Through Him the eyes of our hearts are opened, and our dim and clouded understanding unfolds like a flower to the light; for through Him the Lord permits us to taste the wisdom of eternity.'[2]

The pieces collected in this book – most of which began life as conferences to fellow monks or as homilies in the monastery church – are all occasional, and the order into which they have been cast here makes no claim at anything systematic. They are no more than 'markers' on the Christian way, attempts to say something, while we wait, about 'the gifts that lie within our comprehension'. But if they help stir a fresh sense of the goodness, truth and beauty of these gifts, if they help any to live with understanding and joy the mystery 'which was kept secret for long ages but is now disclosed' (Rom 16:25–6), 'this mystery, which is Christ in you, the hope of glory' (Col 1:27), their author will feel blessed himself.

Every Benedictine monastery is surrounded and supported by lay friends, many of whom will be oblates, taking the *Rule of St Benedict* as a guide for their Christian life in the world and often giving great inspiration to struggling monks. I am happy to dedicate this book to them, as a small tribute to their dedication and kindnesses. And once again, I owe special thanks to Eileen Grant without whom this book, like its predecessor, would never have existed at all.

> Today, as in the days of St Paul, the Christian, no matter how humble or obscure, is the child of God; he exists in Christ, and he possesses the strength of the Holy Spirit. It is inconceivable that the presence of Christ and the action of the Holy Spirit will not reveal themselves in some way, even to those least aware. Furthermore, the life of the Christian is a perpetual renewal and rejuvenation; should he not then appear to be of another race than 'those of the world'? He has a unique dignity: he is master of himself and he is free! He loves his neighbour, shows kindness, compassion, and an untiring devotion towards all. He is always filled with serenity; even when he is being tested, he is jubilant. The harmony of all his moral qualities makes him beautiful and attractive. Others are drawn by his peace, his optimism, his courage, and his happiness. He is gracious to everyone alike, and his sweetness and gentleness win him many hearts. The normal life of Christians does indeed shine like a light in the darkness of the world, and its splendour convinces men of the truth of the faith.[3]

May even something of this be true for us – for the glory of God, for our own consolation and for the healing of the world!

Abbot Hugh Gilbert,
First Sunday of Lent, 2008

Notes

1. St Clement of Rome, *Letter to the Corinthians* 35.
2. Ibid., 36.
3. Ceslaus Spicq, O.P., *Saint Paul and Christian Living* (Gill & Son, Dublin, 1964), pp. 90-1.

Prologue

The Immaculate Conception

Homily 2002

Once one has been a good time in the monastery, one has plenty of things to be embarrassed about. I was once given a tree to plant. I chose a good spot, I thought. I dug a hole, as one does, and put the young tree in it. Time passed, and the tree showed no signs of growth. Indeed, it looked decidedly unhappy. Then along came another monk, as happens, kindly bent on rectifying my incompetence. It turned out I had successfully planted the tree on top of a large rock. Well, the Bible recommends rocks for building houses on, but they're definitely not for trees.

It is a parable in reverse for today. God the Father is a much better gardener than I am. When he's going to plant a tree, he prepares the earth properly. Mary is the earth, and Christ is the tree, the Tree of Life. And the rock is no bad image of original sin.

What is the 'Immaculate Conception'? What does it mean? It means that Mary, from the first moment of her existence, was preserved from original sin. And what is original sin? It is the lack of sanctifying grace, of the indwelling Spirit of God giving us a share in God's own life. In the beginning, humanity was conceived in grace; it began its existence beautiful before God. But sin entered the world; the treasure that should have been handed on generation after generation was lost; and, each one of us now begins his or her life deprived, lacking. That lack is what we mean by original sin. Even when we disobeyed, however, and lost God's friendship, he did not abandon us to sin and death. In the fullness of time, the work of complete restoration begins. One name for its beginning is Mary's Immaculate Conception. Mary, by the sheer unmerited grace of God, was preserved from privation. She lacked the lack. Suddenly, among the stony fields of middle earth, comes this patch of cleared soil: a daughter of Eve free from original sin, and by a further extension of grace, free from all personal sin as well, venial and mortal, even from the inclination to sin. Putting it positively, Mary is creation beginning again. She's conceived, not naked and stripped like us, as it were, but beautifully dressed. She is the uncracked, unsmudged mirror giving back the glory of God without any hesitation or unclarity or distortion. She is, in the hallowed phrase, 'full of grace' (Lk 1:28). She is the most gracious, graceful, grateful person conceivable – grace entails all that. Catholic tradition calls her All-holy, All-beautiful, paradise restored, overflowingly lovely. When St Bernadette remarked, 'When you've seen her, you just want to die to see her again', she was only experiencing what this feast has been saying for a thousand years.

What is the Immaculate Conception? It is Mary herself in her God-given beauty, Mary the Holy Spirit's masterpiece.

And why? Why was she conceived in this way? This is the other question. Why this grace of the Spirit given to Mary? So that the healing, life-giving tree might be planted and grow: Jesus, the Christ, the Son of the Father, the Tree of Life. The ground was dug so deep, every stone and thorn and thistle removed, and the old roots of the tree of sin cleared away, so that this soil might receive the Holy Seed, and the stump of Jesse flower. God was beginning again – in the fullness of time – restoring paradise, re-opening the garden. The soil was prepared to welcome the seed of the Son. First comes Mary conceived immaculate and then, in due time, Jesus conceived by the Holy Spirit in her.

> Faithfulness shall spring from the earth
> and justice look down from heaven.
> The Lord will make us prosper
> and our earth shall yield its fruit (Ps 84:12–13).

The Gospel of the Annunciation is the seed falling on rich soil, the soil of a noble and generous heart (cf. Lk 8:15): 'I am the handmaid of the Lord; let what you have said be done to me' (Lk 1:38, JB). This is the seed that will multiply thirtyfold, sixtyfold, a hundredfold. This is the tree that will grow so large that the birds of the air will nest in its branches. This is the tree of life, that will hang on wood at Calvary and rise from the tomb with fruit in its hands – fruit the Holy Spirit will pass to us from Pentecost on.

Today we're praising Father, Son and Holy Spirit for all of this, in its beginning. The Spirit made Mary immaculate, so that she could welcome the Son, and the Son, through his life, death and resurrection, take us home to the Father's house. How can we not want to be part of this, part of it from the beginning?

In fact, the beginning is in us already. What the Holy Spirit did for Mary in her conception, he does for us, at our level, through our baptism. The rock of the original lack is lifted from our hearts and the seed of grace is set within them. Our hearts, and lives, thus take on a Marian potential. They become a soil where the Tree of Life can take root. The work that remains is just picking out stones, toilsome though it be. It's our free seconding of the cleansing, ploughing, watering action of the Spirit. Currently (2002), how busy the Spirit seems, clearing the soil of the Church, bringing our sins to the surface and a contemptuous public gaze! But always and only so that the soil of the Church and every member of it may be more Marian: a place where the Father can plant the tree of his Son, and this Son grow, flourish and bear fruit. And each of us too, in the Son, become 'like a tree that is planted / beside the flowing waters, / that yields its fruit in due season / and whose leaves shall never fade' (Ps 1:3); leaf-laden, fruit-bearing trees, 'for the healing of the nations' (Rev 22:2).

> O Lord, you once favoured your land
> and revived the fortunes of Jacob,
> you forgave the guilt of your people
> and covered all their sins.
> You averted all your rage,
> you calmed the heat of your anger (Ps 84:2–4).

This is what begins today, pre-emptively in Mary. This is what begins again every Advent and Christmas. It is what begins with our baptism, and begins in our hearts plainly and humbly, day after day, in faith, hope and love. This is what is really going on in the world and in our lives: this work of the God of the garden, Father, Son and Holy Spirit. May each of us yield to it with Mary and say, 'Be it done to me according to your word.'

Part I: Rooted

As therefore you have received Christ Jesus the Lord, live in him, rooted and built up in him and established in the faith, just as you were taught, abounding in thanksgiving (Col 2:6–7).

1

The Christ We Know

I

*That which was from the beginning, which we have heard,
which we have seen with our eyes, which we have looked upon
and touched with our hands, concerning the word of life – the
life was made manifest, and we saw it, and testify to it, and
proclaim to you the eternal life which was with the Father and
was made manifest to us – that which we have seen and heard
we proclaim also to you, so that you may have fellowship with
us; and our fellowship is with the Father and with his Son
Jesus Christ* (1 Jn 1:1–3).

So begins the First Letter of John. It is nothing if not an
evocative passage. It allows us to catch Christianity, as it
were, at the moment of birth. The apostles had encountered
Christ, through their ears and eyes and hands, in a unique and
unrepeatable way. They had felt themselves in the presence of
a definitive, unsurpassable divine revelation; they had given
it, and him, their faith, and had found real, eternal life. And
so they felt obliged to testify to and proclaim to others what
had been manifested to them, so that those others would be led
to believe what they believed of Jesus, and be brought,
through fellowship with them, into the same saving communion with the Father and his Son Jesus Christ. How clear it is,
too, that what is to be conveyed across the generations is
essentially a knowledge of and relationship with the person of
Christ. It's this relationship which is eternal life. Christianity,
in other words, is Christ. Jews, Buddhists, Muslims would be

the first to affirm that Judaism is not Moses nor Buddhism Buddha nor Islam Muhammed, but for Christians Christianity *is* Christ. Even though he does, he doesn't *merely* bring some-thing other than himself, a word or a wisdom or a life. He is himself that word, wisdom, life. Even though he does take us to the Father, he is not merely a pointer, not even merely the way. He is in the Father, he and the Father are one, and 'he who has seen me has seen the Father' (Jn 14:9). Something at least of his unique status is suggested in the mysterious phrase with which John's Letter opens, 'That which was from the beginning'. It inevitably reminds us of the opening of John's Gospel. He is the Word who was in the beginning with God, the full expression of all that God is and, at a specific time and place, he became flesh and dwelt among us. And due to that, 'our fellowship is with the Father and with his Son Jesus Christ'.

Thanks to the Tradition which comes from the Apostles and is transmitted by their successors, the bishops – 'by means of preaching, bearing witness, institutions, worship and inspired writings'[1] – thanks to its supreme embodiment in the celebra-tion and sacrament of the Eucharist, we too, by believing, are able to enter into this 'fellowship' or 'communion' with the Father and the Son, and so find eternal life.

So there opens out for us, and for every generation, the possibility of an experience of Christ, a 'hearing', 'seeing' and 'touching' of him, distinct of course from that of his orig-inal ear- and eye-witnesses, but still real. The First Letter of John calls it, repeatedly, 'knowing'. 'By this we know ...' is a refrain of the Letter. 'And by this we know that he abides in us, by the Spirit which he has given us' (1 Jn 3:24). It is a knowing *within faith*. It is a knowing that confesses the truth of the Incarnation (4:2) and listens to the testimony of author-itative teachers in the Church (4:6). It is a knowing made possible by the 'anointing' received in the beginning (2:20; the gift of the Spirit in baptism is perhaps the reference here). It is intimately connected with keeping the commandments (2:3) and loving the brethren (3:14; 4:7). It is incompatible with sin (3:6). It is a knowing of divine love (3:16; 4:16) and eternal life (3:14; 5:13). It is confidence in prayer (5:15). It is knowing 'that the Son of God has come and has given us understanding' (5:20).

'He who believes in the Son of God has the testimony in himself,' says John (1 Jn 5:10). This testimony is the echo within the heart of the believer of the testimony of the Apostles. In the end, it is the very presence of Christ himself.

> Let him easter in us, be a dayspring to the dimness of us,
>   be a crimson-cresseted east . . .
> Our hearts' charity's hearth's fire, our thoughts' chivalry's
>   throng's Lord.[2]

So runs the prayer with which Hopkins ends 'The Wreck of the Deutschland'. In simpler words perhaps, but in the same sense, any believer may want to pray.

It is this inner knowing, 'sensing', of Christ, his presence in heart and thought, I would like to explore here, with Newman as a first guide.

II

In the final pages of his *Grammar of Assent* (1870) Ven. John Henry Newman takes issue with the aetiology with which Edward Gibbon, in his famous *History of the Decline and Fall of the Roman Empire* (1776–1788), explains (and in a sense explains away) the remarkable rise of Christianity. The causes Gibbon adduces – five in number – go only so far, says Newman, in explaining how Christianity spread so widely in the first centuries, survived persecution and eventually established itself as a dominant social reality in the world of Late Antiquity. The decisive dynamic lies elsewhere. 'A temporal sovereign,' writes Newman,

> makes himself felt by means of his subordinate administrators, who bring his power and will to bear upon every individual of his subjects who personally know him not; the universal Deliverer, long expected, when He came, He too, instead of making and

securing subjects by a visible graciousness or majesty, departs; – *but* is found, through His preachers, to have imprinted the Image or idea of Himself in the minds of His subjects individually; and that Image, apprehended and worshipped in individual minds, becomes a principle of association, and a real bond of those subjects one with another, who are thus united to the body by being united to that Image; and moreover that Image, which is their moral life, when they have already been converted, is also the original instrument of their conversion. It is the Image of Him who fulfils the one great need of human nature, the Healer of its wounds, the Physician of the soul, this Image it is which both creates faith, and then rewards it.[3]

It was this 'Image' that, proclaimed by the Church, provoked conversion and faith, and then lodged in believers as that 'Thought of Christ', a 'mental vision', 'the inward Vision of their Divine Lord', which sustained and inspired them, united them to each other for all their human differences, gave energy to their worship and enabled so many of them, children and slaves included, to accept the loss of their life not only with equanimity but even with joy.

Newman is doing more here than responding to Gibbon, more than 'explaining' the successes of the early Church. He is touching on the inmost inspiration of the Christian believer of any time or place. And this, in his terms, is the 'image' or 'idea' or 'thought' or 'vision' of Christ that he or she carries within. Newman would often quote St Paul's words to Agrippa, referring to his experience outside Damascus: 'I was not disobedient to the heavenly vision' (Acts 26:19). Newman himself felt, in the memorable phrases of his *Apologia*, that he had, at the age of 15, 'received into [his] mind impressions of dogma which, through God's mercy, had never been effaced or obscured'. In other words, through the formulas of Christian Tradition, God himself had impressed upon him a 'vision', an 'image' of his Saviour, which had sustained faith and love within him throughout his life.

Many today may find Newman's language either too cerebral ('idea') or too pictorial ('image'), and prefer to speak of an inner 'knowing' or 'sensing' of Christ, an inner presence or a persistent memory. Language little matters as long as the

one, same reality is in view. And both Johannine 'knowing'
and Newmanian 'vision' are looking to it. Certainly, Newman
does not mean a mere abstract concept of Christ, nor simply
an inner bodily imagining of him composed of reminiscences
of the best or worst of Christian iconography. He means a
real, concrete, direct, vivid, inner apprehension of the Person
of Christ, engaging thought, will, action, and emotions – that
is the whole of ourselves. He means a 'realization' in the mind
and heart of who and what Christ is.

III

In what, though, for the Christian (the Christian, that is, who
stands in the 'Great Tradition' of the apostolic churches) does
this 'vision', this 'realization', this 'knowing' consist? What
is its object or content? It is a knowing, certainly, of Jesus of
Nazareth, the historical figure, not of a mere universal or
Gnostic or spiritual 'Christ'. It is a vision of the Jesus of the
four canonical Gospels: of the Jesus of the Beatitudes, the
Sermon on the Mount, the Lord's Prayer, of the parables, the
healings, the exorcisms, of the Baptism in the Jordan and the
Transfiguration on the mountain. Central to it will be the
figure on the Cross and, as is so clear in the instance of St
Paul, on the One who has risen from the dead and is the
unseen Lord and Judge of history. It is a vision that liturgical
celebration confirms and renews. It is a 'knowing' that will
seek this figure in every human being, and especially in the
'least', the 'little ones', the poor. It will be the realization of
this One as a Saviour, a Friend, a Brother, as the Great Lover,
'who loved me and gave himself for me' (Gal 2:20), and does
so still and always, eucharistically especially, and who is
waiting for me at the end of my earthly life.

But is there more? How can there not be? 'There are,' as
St John of the Cross expressed it, 'depths to be sounded in
Christ, new veins of new riches.' Both heart and mind will
always be asking, Who is he? 'Of you my heart has spoken:
"Seek his face." It is your face, O Lord, that I seek; hide not
your face' (Ps 26:8–9). And the heart, for the Old Testament,

is the seat of thought and will, not merely emotion. It is the whole person who is seeking here. Who is it, then, we are given to 'know' and 'see'? Once again Newman, in a passage from one of his Anglican sermons, can be a guide.

> In truth, until we contemplate our Lord and Saviour, God and man, as a really existing being, external to our minds, as complete and entire in His personality as we show ourselves to be to each other, as one and the same in all His various and contrary attributes, 'the same yesterday, today, and for ever' – we are using words which profit not. Till then we do not realize that Object of faith, which is not a mere name on which titles and properties may be affixed without congruity and meaning, but has a personal existence and an identity distinct from everything else. In what true sense do we 'know' Him, if our idea of Him be not such as to take up and incorporate into itself the manifold attributes and offices which we ascribe to Him? What do we gain from words, however correct and abundant, if they end with themselves, instead of lighting up the image of the Incarnate Son in our heart?[4]

What Newman is saying here, first of all, is that the 'idea' or 'image' of Christ that we carry within must be real. It must refer to things, not words; it must correspond to the reality of who Christ is; it must be true; it must be a valid sacrament, as it were, of what it represents. It must truly 'know'. And further, it must be able to hold together the many contrasting facets of Christ as he is brought before us by the many voices of Scripture and Tradition. It must be able to incorporate into itself such strange antinomies as Jewish rabbi and universal Saviour, servant of the Lord and Lord of lords, death and resurrection, humanity and divinity. It must be coherent; it must have a synthesizing power. Only thus will this 'image' be a 'beginning' or a 'dayspring' within us, both a place of contemplative rest and a spring of action. Only thus will it give life, able to grow with us and be a source of growth for us.

Once again, then, Who ultimately is Jesus of Nazareth? Who is the crucified and risen One? Who is my Saviour and my Lover? To echo Jesus' own question, 'Who do *we* say the

Son of man is?' In Matthew's account of that exchange, Peter's answer ends, 'the *Son* of the living God.' The Johannine passage with which we began comes to rest at the same place: 'and our fellowship is with the Father and with *his Son* Jesus Christ.' The answer at which Newman himself arrived, through his own reading of the Bible and the Fathers of the early Church and in conflict with the inadequacies of both the liberal and evangelical Christologies of his day, was the same. It is disclosed in the title he gave the sermon from which the above passage was taken: 'The Humiliation of the *Eternal Son*'. For Newman, Jesus is at root – in the beginning – the Son of God, in the strict and ultimate, classical and 'high', sense of the phrase. It is, in his own phrase, 'the image of the Incarnate *Son*' that the Holy Spirit wants to light up in our hearts.

'We have, perhaps,' says Newman,

> a vague general notion that [the words 'Son of God'] mean something extraordinary and supernatural; but we know that we ourselves are called, in one sense, sons of God in Scripture. Moreover, we have heard, perhaps ... that the Angels are sons of God. In consequence, we collect just thus much from the title as applied to our Lord, that He came from God, that He was the well-beloved of God, and that He is much more than a mere man. This is all that the words convey to many men at the most; while many more refer them merely to His human nature. How different is the state of those who have been duly initiated into the mysteries of the kingdom of heaven! How different was the mind of the primitive Christians, who so eagerly and vigorously apprehended the gracious announcement, that in this title, 'The Son of God', they saw and enjoyed the full glories of the Gospel doctrine! When times grew cold and unbelieving, then indeed, as at this day, public explanations were necessary of those simple and sacred words; but the first Christians needed none. They felt that in saying that Christ was the Son of God, they were witnessing to a thousand marvellous and salutary truths, which they could not indeed understand, but by which they might gain life, and for which they could dare to die.[5]

In other words, they had within them a true 'image' or 'idea' or 'vision' of who Christ is.

Again, then, Newman says:

> We speak of Him in a vague way as God, which is true, but not
> the whole truth; and in consequence when we proceed to consider
> His humiliation [i.e. his human experience, and especially his
> suffering and death], we are unable to carry on the notion of His
> personality from heaven to earth. He who was but now spoken of
> as God, without mention of the Father from whom He is, is next
> described as a creature; but how do these distinct notions of Him
> hold together in our minds? We are able to continue the idea of
> a Son into that of a servant, though the descent was infinite, and,
> to our reason, incomprehensible; but when we merely speak first
> of God, then of man, we seem to change the Nature without
> preserving the Person.

And so to the almost understated, but resolute conclusion:

> In truth, His Divine Sonship is that portion of the sacred doctrine
> on which the mind is providentially intended to rest throughout,
> and so preserve for itself His identity unbroken. But when we
> abandon this gracious help offered to our faith, how can we hope
> to gain the one true and simple vision of Him? How shall we
> possibly look beyond our own words, or apprehend, in any sort,
> what we say?[6]

Newman's quest for a true image of Jesus of Nazareth, his
search for his face, led him, then, to 'His Divine Sonship'.
There lies the heart of Jesus' identity: he is the eternal Son
of the eternal Father. He is the 'only-begotten Son, who is
in the bosom of the Father' (Jn 1:18), God from God, Light
from Light, begotten not made, and who became flesh and
dwelt among us in the days of Herod and Pilate. It is the
Son of God who is, so to speak, the subject of the sentence
of which incarnation, birth, baptism, temptation, preaching
of the kingdom, arrest, condemnation, crucifixion, burial,
death, resurrection, ascension and return in glory are the
predicate. It is the Son of God who is the actor in the play,
the protagonist in the story, the hero of the narrative. It is
the Son who is at once the crucified and risen One, at once
human and divine. Everything in him is held together by,

everything flows from, his being as Son, his divine Person. 'Heart speaks to heart', Newman believed, and the heart can only be satisfied with the vision of a *person*. It was, thus, in the 'vision' or 'image' or 'idea' of the divine Person of the Son, the second Person of the Three in One, that Newman's heart came to rest. There he found the principle of unity. There he found at the same time 'that which was from the beginning' and the beginning and dayspring of his own dedicated Christian life.

IV

Here many popular oppositions – for example between the personal and the ecclesial – fall away. Here, rather, emerges a parallelism (of which Newman himself was certainly aware) between the movement of the pondering heart of the Christian and the broader movement of Christian thought, of Christological inquiry, in the early centuries of the Church. The movement from multiplicity to a unity (which at least if properly conceived doesn't cancel the multiplicity but integrates it), the quest for a coherent, synthesized vision, made by an individual like Newman, echoes at its level the journey of early Christianity. Ontogenesis and phylogenesis, microcosm and macrocosm, correspond to each other.

The pluralism of the New Testament witness to Jesus is a commonplace of contemporary scholarship. 'Probably the first thing that strikes us [regarding the New Testament's presentation of Christ] is the enormous diversity of the testimony given,' writes the Anglican theologian John Macquarrie.[7] Indeed, according to Balthasar, 'there has to be a plurality of New Testament theologies; only thus can they give an idea of the transcendence of the one they proclaim.'[8] Yes, it's a salutary fact. The New Testament writers offer us 'images, pictures, metaphors ... not strictly defined concepts, but allusive ideas with somewhat blurred edges.' And so one can hardly disagree when Macquarrie says: 'When one is dealing with images of this sort, it is not desirable to set up one of them as normative, and to eliminate all the others.'[9]

Are we misguided, though, to seek for a unity to this diversity or a pattern for the plurality? Surely not. Faith seeks understanding, and to understand is to unify. The Church has sought, constantly seeks, such a unified understanding, and so does the pondering heart. There is, after all, the plain, objective fact to which St Cyril of Alexandria is the great historical witness: Christ is one. Our affirmations about the Lord will always be paradoxical, but needn't be incoherent. He will always surpass us, but still, like St Paul, we can know the One we believe in, and what we know, for all its unsearchable richness, is always a unity. We are seeking a Face.

In an essay of 1981, Joseph Ratzinger traced the way in which the early Church came to 'read' the multifarious apostolic testimony to Jesus:

> In concrete terms, the struggle to arrive at a proper understanding of Christ in the primitive Church is the struggle to sift [the many] titles of Jesus and put them in the correct perspective and order. In short, the whole process can be described as one of increasing simplification and concentration. In the end only three titles remain as the community's valid adumbration of the mystery of Jesus: Christ, Lord and Son (of God). [But] since the title Christ (Messiah) became more and more associated with the name Jesus and had little clear meaning outside a Jewish milieu; and since Lord too, was not as clear as 'Son', a further concentration took place: the title 'Son' comes in the end to be the only comprehensive designation for Jesus. It both comprises and interprets everything else. So, finally, the Church's confession of faith can be satisfied with this title ... In bringing the many strands of tradition together in this one word and thus imparting an ultimate simplicity to the fundamental Christian option, the Church was not oversimplifying and reducing; in the word 'Son' she had found that simplicity which is both profound and all-embracing ... making everything else accessible and intelligible.[10]

Similarly Bernard Lonergan, taking the story on to the Council of Nicea (AD 325), affirms: 'The Nicene dogma marks a transition from a multiplicity of symbols, titles and predicates, to the ultimate ground of these, namely the Son's consubstantiality with the Father.'[11] And this is no betrayal.

As Ratzinger remarks, 'Calling Jesus the "Son", far from overlaying him with the mythical gold of dogma ... corresponds most strictly to the centre of the historical figure of Jesus. For the entire gospel testimony is unanimous that Jesus' words and deeds flowed from his most intimate communion with the Father.'[12]

In other words, in those early centuries and after much theological strife, the mind of the whole Church came to rest providentially in the thought, the idea, the vision of Christ as the Son of God. And so the central, Christological section of the Nicene-Constantinopolitan Creed we sing every Sunday begins: 'And in one Lord Jesus Christ, the only-begotten *Son of God*, God from God, Light from Light, true God from true God, begotten not made, of one being with the Father, who ...' did and suffered all that the Gospels and New Testament tell of him. Again, the subject of the sentence, the principle of unity, the true *dramatis persona*, the essential point of reference and the ultimate focus of Christian worship and life has been uncovered; the beginning and the dayspring. It is / he is the Son of God.

It is worth briefly adding that between the two great Ecumenical Councils of Chalcedon (AD 451) and Constantinople II (AD 553), and amid different challenges, the same trajectory was relived. The Council of Chalcedon, responding to a misinterpretation of Alexandrine Christology, had emphasized especially the duality of natures, divine and human, in the one person or 'hypostasis' of Christ. He was fully, truly, completely God, and fully, truly, completely man, consubstantial with the Father by virtue of the first and consubstantial with us by virtue of the second. But this could be (perversely) taken to imply that the 'person' of Christ was simply the end-product, the conflation so to speak, of a coming together of two autonomous natures. It was this possible misinterpretation that the next Council, Constantinople II, had to lay to rest. It did so by clarifying that in Jesus, the person or 'hypostasis' is not the 'product' or 'result' of the two 'natures', but their 'subject', their ground and source, and that this hypostasis is to be identified unequivocally with the Second Person of the Trinity, with the eternal Son. It was, in the famous formula of the Council, 'One of the Trinity', that is the eternal Son, who 'was crucified for us'. The mystery of the Incarnation consists in the 'taking on' by the eternal Son of the Father of a human nature and therefore a human history. 'Thus everything in Christ's human nature is to be attributed to his divine person as its proper subject, not only his miracles but also his sufferings and even his death' (*Catechism* 468), and it is because of this – because of what the theologians call the 'hypostatic union' – that the mysteries of his life, death and resurrection are able to rescue and transform us, and bring us into communion with himself and the Father. The divine personality does not, for an instant, imply the diminution of his humanity, but rather its enhancement and empowerment, its elevation to the status of *instrumentum salutis*.

Once again, then, Christian experience, corporate as well as individual, brings us back to the starting-point: to the image of Christ as the Son of God. 'And we *know*,' says John, 'that the *Son of God* has come' (1 Jn 5:20).

V

Isn't all this, though, a disastrous and unnecessary disconnection from the 'simple Christ' of the Gospels? I think not. And what does it have to do with the simple, believing, praying Christian? It may help him.

I have never forgotten the sad remark of a biblical exegete commenting on the Gospel portraits of Christ, and saying, 'I always have this hang-up at the back of my mind that Christ is God.' This was precisely the misunderstanding Newman was addressing in the homily quoted above, the misunderstanding that arises from beginning from 'nature' rather than 'person'. Had our exegete realized that Christ is the *Son*, his divine Sonship now expressing or realizing itself also at the human level, in a human fashion, in a human life wholly turned towards the Father and wholly devoted to the mission given him by the Father, his sense of awkwardness would have dissolved. Nothing emerges more clearly from the

Gospels, as Joseph Ratzinger pointed out in the essay mentioned above, than 'the centre of the life and person of Jesus is his constant communication with the Father'.[13] To centre on the divine Sonship of Jesus is to give primacy to his relationship with the Father. It is to acknowledge that *his* 'centre' was (and is) Another. The first words the twelve-year-old Jesus speaks in the Gospel of Luke are, 'Did you not know that I must be about my *Father's* business?' (Lk 2:49, NKJ). Nothing, again, is clearer from the New Testament witness than that 'Jesus died praying' and, at the Last Supper and on the Cross, was in prayer 'transforming his death, from within, into an act of love, into a glorification of God'.[14] The last words of the dying Jesus in the Gospel of Luke are, '*Father*, into your hands I commend my spirit' (Lk 23:46). The Jesus of the Gospels, the Jesus of the most primitive imaginable testimony as well as of the most elaborated, is clearly someone in a unique relationship with the Father, living his whole life and dying his death entirely within that relationship – 'Abba, Father!' – only to be 'begotten' anew by the Father in his resurrection, to have his Sonship vindicated: 'You are my Son; today I have begotten you.'

And this 'image', 'idea', 'vision' of Christ, the Son of God, is not only faithful to the Gospels, it brings us to the heart of *the* Gospel. It brings us in turn to communion with the Father and the Son, as St John described it. As the New Testament repeatedly expresses it, to be a Christian, to be a baptized believer, is to be reborn, to become a child, a son or daughter, of God, a 'son in the Son'. 'You have been born anew, not of perishable seed but of imperishable,' says Peter (1 Pet 1:23). 'For in Christ Jesus,' says Paul, 'you are all sons of God, through faith' (Gal 3:26). 'To all who received him,' says John, 'who believed in his name, he gave power to become children of God' (Jn 1:12). 'Every one who believes that Jesus is the Christ is a child of God' (1 Jn 5:1). To be a Christian is to be 'in Christ' and therefore allotted a share in Christ's, the Son's, relationship to the Father. It is to have Christ as one's 'centre', and thus to be 'de-centred' with him, and 're-centred' on the Father. It is to follow the divine Son's human journey to the Father through death and resurrection, to be drawn by the Holy Spirit into the Son's obedient self-giving to the Father for our salvation, to share his prayer, for – Joseph Ratzinger again – 'Since the centre of the person of Jesus is prayer, it is essential to participate in his prayer if we are to know and understand him.'[15] It is to enter into what is the very heart and centre of Christ himself, his relationship as 'beloved Son' to the Father. To be a Christian, as we experience at every Eucharist, is to be able to stand with our brothers and sisters and pray the prayer that only Jesus, the Son, could have taught us – 'Our Father' – and in the silence of our hearts to hear the Father say to us too, 'This is my beloved Son, with whom I am well pleased' (Mt 3:17).

To accept the Tradition that comes to us from the Apostles, to share the faith of the Church, is, then, to pass through a door into that 'fellowship with the Father and with his Son Jesus Christ' of which John speaks. It is, like Paul, to 'know whom I have believed' (2 Tim 1:12). It is to have a relationship with Christ. It is to carry within oneself, as a beginning and a dayspring, an 'image', a 'vision' of him. And this 'him', as the Holy Spirit who leads the whole Church and each believer, will progressively reveal, is before all else, and in all that he is and does, the Son. It is 'the image of the Incarnate Son' that the Holy Spirit lights up in our hearts. His death and resurrection, his paschal mystery, at its deepest level is the supreme expression in the human of that Sonship. His relationship to myself and to others, as Healer and Friend, Saviour and Lover, is grounded in another and prior relationship, which gives it all its fullness, that of the Son to the Father. And so to 'know' and 'see' him, hear and touch him, love and commune with him, to eat his Body and drink his Blood, is to be taken up into what is most his own, his divine Sonship, his eternal relationship with the Father.

Thus John ends his Letter: 'And we know that the Son of God has come and has given us understanding, to know him who is true; and we are in him who is true, in his Son Jesus Christ. This is the true God and eternal life. Little children, keep yourselves from idols' (1 Jn 5:10–21).

Notes

1. *Compendium of the Catechism of the Catholic Church* 12 (CTS, London, 2006).
2. G. M. Hopkins, 'The Wreck of the Deutschland', from *Poems* (4th ed., 1967), ed. W. H. Gardner & N. H. MacKenzie (OUP, Oxford), p. 51.
3. J. H. Newman, *A Grammar of Assent* (Uni. Notre Dame, Notre Dame/London, 1979), p. 359.
4. J. H. Newman, *Parochial and Plain Sermons* III, 12 (Longmans, London, 1901), pp. 169–70
5. Ibid., pp. 161–2.
6. Ibid., pp. 170–1.
7. John Macquarrie, *Jesus Christ in Modern Thought* (SCM Press, London, 1990), p. 142.
8. H. U. von Balthasar, *Theodrama* III (Ignatius Press, San Francisco, 1998), p. 144.
9. Macquarrie, p. 143.
10. Joseph Ratzinger, *Behold the Pierced One* (Ignatius Press, San Francisco, 1986), pp. 16–17.
11. Bernard Lonergan, *The Way to Nicea* (DLT, London, 1982), p. 136.
12. Ratzinger, p. 17.
13. Ibid., p. 15.
14. Ibid., p. 22.
15. Ibid., p. 25.

2

Baptism

In Search of the Centre

'*Blessed is he who comes in the name of the Lord.*' When a
child is born, we talk of it as 'having entered the world'. And
so with our Lord at Christmas, but with a whole new level of
meaning: now the Son of God, a divine Person, enters the
world as a human baby. At Epiphany, though, it's not so
much the world he comes to as the Church, the Church made
up of Jew and Gentile, and now wedded to the Lord. Today,
at the end of the Christmas season, it's as if, by way of the
sacrament of Baptism, he comes to each of us. 'Blessed is he
who comes' – first to the world, then to the Church, then to
each one of us. 'The giant of twofold substance' (St Ambrose)
getting closer step by step ... 'Blessed is he who comes in the
name of the Lord' – and today to each of us. Each of us went
into the Jordan and out again when we were baptized.

And so a great question surfaces here: what does it mean to
be a Christian? Or, what is the Christian life? It *is* a great
question. It's a great question for each of us. We need to
answer it adequately if we're going to live something
approaching an adequate Christian life. *Da mihi intellectum ut
sciam testimonia tua!* 'Give me understanding that I may know
your commands.' Without adequate understanding, derived
from sound Christian doctrine, Christian life will be an attenuated life, will wither even. Without the on-going self-
catechesis of *lectio divina*, our Christian life will be
attenuated. It won't reach its full potential. The question, what
is the Christian life?, is then a great question. And not just for
each of us, but also for the Church's mission, for the re-evan-

gelization of our Western world. A true and vibrant presentation of what being a Christian and living the Christian life mean will surely tend to convince, and conversely. History shows it. The Apostles and the Fathers preached the full, true idea of Christianity, and the fruit was martyrs, monks, mystics. Islam, on the other hand, arose in an environment permeated by a defective Christianity. Secularism arose because the witness to the Christian life had been impaired by division. The revival of religious life in the Church of England in the last century (of which our community is an indirect heir) arose because, even within the uncertain world of Anglicanism, the Oxford Movement preached a true theology of the Christian life.

It is a matter of finding our way back to the Christian centre.

Misconceptions or reduced conceptions abound, and a preliminary clearing of the ground does no harm. First, one might mention moralism. At the Mass of Christmas Night, a section of the Letter to Titus is read. It includes the sentence, in the Jerusalem Bible version: 'We must be self-restrained and live good and religious lives here in this present world' (Tit 2:12). This is paraphrase, not translation and, I must confess, it doesn't lift my heart. Be teetotal, nice, and go to church, it seems to suggest. Was it for this the Son of God became one of us? There are many people in our society who do think of themselves as, in some sense, residually Christian. They are not antipathetic to Christianity, but they're well aware of not being fully or denominationally committed. And if they were asked what, in their view, being a Christian would entail, they might well answer rather like that translation of that reading. And that is precisely why they stay as they are. It is hardly a ravishing vision. Being a Christian, living the Christian life, would be – in this view – a compound of self-restraint, being honest in business and tax-returns and so on, going to church on Sundays perhaps and generally being 'nice' to people. It means being 'moral', being 'good' – and getting to heaven as a result. This is bourgeois Christianity, really. It exists in an

Anglican form, in Presbyterian and Nonconformist forms and *mutatis mutandis* in a Catholic form: the 'good Catholic', the one who keeps the rules. The author of *The Cruelty of Heresy*[1] pointed in this connection to the great influence in the Anglo-Saxon world of *The Whole Duty of Man,* an anonymous work dated to the mid-seventeenth century: Christianity as a keeping of the law, as a moral enterprise, and really nothing else. A more attractive variant of this: Christianity equals the selfless service of others, and really nothing else. This is actually more inspiring and currently fashionable, but it is no less a half-truth.

Misconception number two: asceticism. This may not be walking the streets at the present time, but it has a long history of doing so. Since the time of the Desert Fathers, Christianity has begotten an immense literature on how to live a committed, serious Christian life – in the cloister or outside. This literature, broadly speaking, has been a gift of the vowed, religious life to the rest of the Church. More precisely, a great deal of ascetical literature actually comes from novice masters! And we know the major themes: the three ways, spiritual warfare, the practice of the virtues, prayer – with, in some schools, an opening to an eventual mysticism. Our own Rule, of course, is one of the classics of this literature (though not simply reducible to it); so are the *Institutes* and *Conferences* of Cassian, the *Imitation of Christ*, the *Spiritual Exercises* of St Ignatius, the *Spiritual Combat* of Lorenzo Scupoli, the *Introduction to the Devout Life* of St Francis de Sales and so on. For the Eastern Orthodox, there's the *Philokalia*. In our own time, there's a proliferation of books on 'spirituality' or 'psycho-spirituality', which are the contemporary equivalents. Here we have more than the moral: a pursuit of the 'holy', the 'spiritual', having a 'spiritual life', being on a 'spiritual journey'. One might think, surely this isn't a misconception at all. Indeed. The weakness, though, lies in what is omitted. Omitted perhaps, because taken for granted – but still omitted, and therefore forgettable. The underlying vision of what being a Christian means, what living the Christian life means, can be less than fully theological. The exposition is determined by the practical concerns of the author, and so tends to use the language of morality, spirituality, psychology or whatever. The centre of interest will be us: our attitudes, our state of soul, our maturity, our love or whatever, depending on the period and the author's general thrust. God's all-embracing plan, the 'mystery', will tend to be background merely. In the days when the broad outlines of the biblical story and the great doctrinal truths filled the air, this hardly mattered. But those days are not ours.

Misconception number three we might call pietism. It is Christianity as personal experience: that of being forgiven and saved, for example in the evangelical view; that of being spoken to by the Lord and filled with the Spirit, in the charismatic view. It may be reaction against misconceptions one and two, an attempt to reaffirm the primacy of grace against any latent Pelagianism. One wonders if preoccupation with apparitions and heavenly messages isn't another, Catholic version of this.

So, misconception one: the reduction of Christian living to good behaviour; misconception two: the reduction of Christian living to asceticism and spirituality; misconception three: the reduction of Christian living to felt experience. And, as always, it is less what is affirmed that is askew, which is often indeed an essential part of the whole, but more the one-sidedness. Morality, spirituality, personal experience all have their place in Christianity. But the centre, on which they depend, from which they flow, which allots them their proper space, is somewhere else.

Here we are still on the banks of the Jordan, and wondering, what is the true conception? Where is the centre? Christ comes out of the water with the Spirit resting on him and the Voice of the Father thunders above him: This is my Son, the Beloved. No single mystery of Christ's, of course, even less any conceptual formulation, can say exhaustively what needs to be said. And yet here, in this scene, we have a true icon, and we can say: yes, there is a true vision of Christianity, and it can be – however haltingly – expressed. Better, there is a reality in which, believing and baptized, we already are and into which we can be ever more drawn. Being a Christian means being 'in Christ'. Living the Christian life means living 'in Christ' or living the Christ-life. Christian life is 'mystical' not simply in its goal, in its fullness, but from the beginning and in its essence.

What opens out before us – from the Incarnation on, from the Lord's baptism on – then becomes something vast, divine, thrilling. It is something other than moral rectitude or conformity to the will of God or psychological maturity or spiritual profundity or emotional security. It is 'sonship in the Son', being sons and daughters of the Father through the Spirit, sharers in the divine nature, and sharers with the crucified and risen Christ of God's love for the world. It is the Father's love drawing us into the likeness of his Son.

Once we touch this centre, we are in touch with everything: with the Trinity in its distinction of persons, with our own humanity, with humanity as such, with the Church and the sacraments, with Mary, with every human being, with creation. The way of love, sacrificial love to the end, lies wide open before us, as before our Lord today. And morality, spirituality, experience all find their true, derivative place. The Eucharist, the Mass, is the great ritual embodiment of this reality.

Being what we are, we need John the Baptists to bring us to the Jordan and point us to the Lamb of God who takes away the sin of the world (Jn 1:29). We need Johns of Patmos to show us the Lamb standing as if slain in the midst of the Throne (Rev 5:6). We need to see the vision of the true visionaries. The Apostles, Paul and John pre-eminently; the Fathers, perhaps the Alexandrines especially, but not forgetting Augustine and Leo or, indeed, any of them; the Liturgy, Christmas and above all Easter: these are the best of guides.

When Newman began to preach to his Anglican congregations in the 1820s and 1830s, he was in full reaction against both the Evangelicals and the superficial Christianity of the Mammon-serving middle classes. And he actually said, in a letter, that what the age needed was not the 'Gospel', the proclamation of God's merciful love, but the 'Law', the proposition of the hard, practical demands of the Christian way. But he changed. And as his understanding of the Fathers, and of SS John and Paul, deepened, he began to preach more and more this 'high' doctrine of Christian identity and Christian life. It was a significant change and choice, and he gave it unforgettable expression in passages of his *Parochial and Plain Sermons* and his 1838 *Lectures on Justification*. He was anticipating a movement within Christianity as a whole. For a movement there has been, of bringing Christian living back to its objective centre, bringing spirituality and morality back to liturgy and doctrine, reintegrating the peripheral, seeing the Mystery as a whole and living from it.

Other prophets have arisen too, in Newman's wake. To recall the Catholic ones is not to overlook the convergences in other Christian traditions, or the refreshing influence of twentieth-century Orthodoxy. There was the French Carmelite, Bl. Elisabeth of the Trinity, with her awareness of the indwelling of the Three and a prayer such as this:

> O my beloved Christ ... I ask you to clothe me with yourself, to identify my soul with all the movements of your soul, to immerse me in yourself, to take possession of me, to substitute yourself for me so that my life may be but a radiance of your life ... O consuming Fire, Spirit of love, come upon me so that there may be brought about in my soul a kind of incarnation of the Word: that I may be for him an additional humanity in which he renews the whole of his mystery. And You, O Father, bend down towards your poor little creature, 'overshadow' her, see in her only the Beloved in whom you are well pleased.

There was the Irish Benedictine, Bl. Columba Marmion, whose mission it was to re-centre the understanding of the Christian life on Christ, as the titles of his books were at pains to make clear: *Christ in his Mysteries*, *Christ the Life of the Soul*, *Christ the Ideal of the Monk*, *Christ the Ideal of the Priest*.

> The divine sonship, which is in Christ by nature, and makes him God's own and only Son, the Only-begotten who is in the bosom of the Father, is to be extended to us by grace, so that in the thought of God Christ is the first-born of many brethren, who are by grace what he is by nature, sons of God: 'he predestined us to be conformed to the image of his Son so that he might be the first-

born of many brethren.' We are here at the central point of the divine plan ... God sent his Son, says St Paul, that we might receive the adoption of sons.[2]

There were the pioneers and perfecters of the theology of the Church as the Mystical Body of Christ, the re-discoverers of Pauline and Johannine theology, the editors of the Fathers, and the protagonists of the liturgical movement, with its focus on the paschal mystery. How can a Benedictine not hail Odo Casel or Anselm Stolz? Then came Vatican II's *Lumen Gentium,* and the Christocentric humanism of *Gaudium et Spes* and John Paul II, with their refrain: 'It is only in the mystery of the Word made flesh that the mystery of man becomes truly clear.' In the liturgical domain, Easter's centrality has been reaffirmed, and the Rite of Christian Initiation for Adults has tried to build Christian formation around it. The centrality of Easter means the centrality of the life in Christ. The marvellous book of that name (*The Life in Christ*) by the fourteenth-century Byzantine layman, Nicholas Cabasilas, can be taken down from the shelf. The Christian life is nothing other than the living out of the Christ-life mediated through the Easter sacraments. If the plot can still be lost, as it clearly can, it is not for want of being articulated.

'For me to live is Christ' (Phil 1:21). This is the centre that beckons us. Little things and great things, suffering and good things, the altar and the sink, life and death all find their place within and around it. Today Christ, disclosed by the Father, anointed by the Spirit, comes up from the water, as he will come up from the tomb. He comes to claim the Church as his Bride, to bring humanity into a new relationship with the Father and with itself. May this, may he, the truth of him, come into our understandings too, and show us what it means to be Christian, to live a Christian life! It is no small thing.

The *Catechism* quotes St John Eudes:

I ask you to consider that our Lord Jesus Christ is your true head, and that you are one of his members. He belongs to you as the head belongs to its members; all that is his is yours: his spirit, his heart, his body and soul and all his faculties. You must make use of all these as of your own, to serve, praise, love, glorify God. You belong to him, as members belong to their head. And so he longs for you to use all that is in you, as if it were his own, for the service and glory of the Father[3] (1698).

Notes

1. C. FitzSimons Allison, *The Cruelty of Heresy* (SPCK, London, 1994).
2. Columba Marmion, *Christ the Life of the Soul*, 2nd edn (Sands & Co., London, 1925), p. 35.
3. St John Eudes, Tract. *de admirabili corde Jesu* 1, 5.

3

The Holy Spirit

Homily for Pentecost

On the third day after his crucifixion, Jesus rose from the dead. Over forty more days he revealed himself to his disciples until the day he was taken up into heaven, the day of his Ascension. And then on the fiftieth day after his Resurrection, the day we're now celebrating, he sent from his Father the Holy Spirit he had promised.

We heard the account of this in the first reading, from the Acts of the Apostles. It was the Jewish feast of Pentecost, fifty days after Passover. The apostles 'were all together in one place', in Jerusalem, 'when suddenly they heard a sound like a powerful wind from heaven, and something appeared to them that seemed like tongues of fire', settling on each (Acts 2:1–3, JB). This sounding wind and the tongues of fire were outward signs of an inner grace. 'They were all filled with the Holy Spirit,' says St Luke (2:4). And this inner grace then made itself known in a miracle: 'They began to speak foreign languages as the Spirit gave them the gift of speech' (2:4).

The wind blew away all the chaff in the disciples' lives, and the fire burned up everything in them that wasn't a part of love. The sound of the wind became the sound of the Word, and the burning tongues became the proclamation of the Gospel.

There was a crowd there, come up to Jerusalem for the feast. They were people from every part of the known world, a symbol of the whole of humanity. They heard the apostles using their own languages. They heard Peter explaining what was happening, how this out-pouring of the Holy Spirit was a sign that God the Father had raised the crucified Jesus, vindicating him, and establishing him as humanity's true Lord. They heard, and to the number of three thousand believed and were baptized. They were baptized for the forgiveness of their sins, and they too received the gift of the Holy Spirit.

It's this we're celebrating today: this coming of the Spirit, this inner transformation, this first preaching of the Gospel, the first baptisms, the forgiveness of sins, the birth of the Church, the completion of the revelation of God, Father, Son and Holy Spirit.

'Alleluia', went this morning's Invitatory, 'the Spirit of the Lord has filled the whole world. Come, let us adore, alleluia!'

This isn't something little. Nor is it something lost in the past.

No, it is not something little. Christmas, Easter, Pentecost: we know that sequence. They're our three great feasts. Our Lord was born, he lived a human life, he grew, at the age of thirty he began to proclaim the coming of God's Kingdom, and this brought him to the Cross. He died, he rose, he ascended into heaven and took his seat at the right hand of the Father. That is the story. But why? For what purpose? Why Christmas? Why Easter? Pentecost is the answer. Everything Jesus did he did 'in the Spirit', moved by the Spirit, and he did it all so that the Spirit might come upon us. 'It is to your advantage that I go away,' he said at the Last Supper, 'for if I do not go away, the Counsellor will not come to you; but if I go, I will send him to you' (Jn 15:7). The Holy Spirit, the third Person of the Blessed Trinity, 'the Lord and Giver of life' as we call him in the Creed, comes today as the fruit of Christ's mission, the completion of his paschal mystery. Christ 'was put to death for our trespasses and rose again for our justification' (Rom 4:25), and it is the Holy Spirit, through baptism and the other sacraments, who brings us that justification, that being-made-right-with-God: the forgiveness of sins and the life of grace. It's he who enables us to live Christ-like lives. It's he who gathers people of every nation together, brings them to faith, brings them into the Church and reconciles the world with God. No, this isn't a little thing, a little postscript to the story of Jesus. It's rather what every-

thing leads up to. The Father sent his Son into the world so
that through the Son the Spirit might transform the world.

It isn't a little thing. And it isn't a past thing either. It
wasn't just for the twelve or one hundred and twenty disciples
(cf. Acts 1:15), or just for those first three thousand believers
(cf. Acts 2:41). *Nunc quoque*, says the Collect we pray today.
'Now too'. 'Now too pour out this same Spirit into the hearts
of believers and through them into the whole world.' We
believe and have been baptized for the forgiveness of sins.
'For by one Spirit we were all baptized into one body' (1 Cor
12:13). We have been confirmed, sealed with the gift of the
Holy Spirit: 'he has put his seal upon us and given us his
Spirit in our hearts as a guarantee' (2 Cor 1:22). We have our
post-baptismal sins forgiven in the sacrament of reconciliation: 'Receive the Holy Spirit. If you forgive the sins of any,
they are forgiven; if you retain the sins of any, they are
retained' (Jn 20:22–3). We eat the Body of Christ, which is
broken to release the Spirit it contains. We are given the Spirit
to drink, says St Paul (cf. 1 Cor 12:13). 'When we cry,
"Abba! Father!" it is the Spirit himself bearing witness with
our spirit that we are children of God' (Rom 8:15–16). When
'we do not know how to pray as we ought, the Spirit himself
intercedes for us' (Rom 8:26). And each of us can say with St
Paul, 'the law of the Spirit of life in Christ Jesus has set me
free from the law of sin and death' (Rom 8:2).

So we too, *nos quoque*, and *nunc quoque*, now too, we have
been given the Gift. And every year this feast renews it. We
have been filled, and we can be filled more and more with the
Holy Spirit, *dulcis hospes animae*, the 'sweet guest of the
soul'. What is it that makes the human being a complete
human being? Not body and soul alone. Body and soul alone
cannot inherit the kingdom of God. But if body and soul are
filled with the Holy Spirit, we are as God intended us to be.
'For the kingdom of God does not mean food and drink but
righteousness and peace and joy in the Holy Spirit' (Rom
14:17).

The Holy Spirit is not an option, but our deepest need.

'In the humility of the flesh and of faith', as the *Catechism*
beautifully says (732), the Spirit is ours. In the humility of our

worries and our hesitations and our irritations, in the humility of our limited energies, in the humility even of suffering, the Spirit is ours. Our Friend, Helper, Advocate, Counsellor, Comforter. Glory be to the Holy Spirit! He enables us to live Christ-like lives, to see as Christ sees. He takes us back, day after day, to the death and the Resurrection of Christ. He takes us back to his own source, the Father and the Son. In the humility of the flesh and of faith, he opens up the path of patient love. He sends us to one another as comforters ourselves. He gives us our share, humble but real, in the mission of Christ and the Church.

Come then, Holy Spirit, fill the hearts of us, your faithful, and kindle in us the fire of your love! Father, send forth Your Spirit and renew the face of the earth! Glory be to the Father and to the Son and to the Holy Spirit!

4

The Way of the Church

Recently at Mass we were hearing the Letter to the Hebrews. One commentator has summed up its view of the Christian life as follows:

> *The pilgrim People of God.* Those to whom the Letter was written were a community of displaced persons. After the pattern of Israel crossing the desert to get to the Promised Land, they shared in the normal condition of spiritual life: they were a people on the move (13:9), pilgrims on earth (11:13), refugees (6:18), or nomads (11:9), progressing towards the solidly-built (12:22; 13:14) city of the living God, or better towards the heavenly Holy of holies (9:8; 10:19); getting closer to it by the day (11:6; 12:18–22), as in a liturgical procession towards the throne of grace (4:16). To believe in God is to approach him so as to offer him worship (12:28). Christians are those who 'draw near' (7:25; 10:1), being qualified to enter the sanctuary and to officiate there (10:14); uprooted here below, but rooted in what is above. In the eyes of a believer, earthly life is an exodus, a perpetual migration. And this exodus is defined by a) the word or revelation of God which lays down the goal and promises rest as a reward for the expenditure of effort and the acceptance of sacrifice; b) providential trials, 'temptations' (2:8; 12:5–11), which seem to be opposed to the realization of hope (10:23), but which are in reality occasions of manifesting that faithfulness by which one pleases God (11:2, 4, 5, 39); it is a matter of crossing a desert, that is to say, a hostile world, full of dangerous circumstances; c) to conquer the difficulties, one must not be isolated, but always remain incorporated in the 'people of God' (4:9) and a 'sharer in Christ' (3:14), who is the head and guide of the corporate

pilgrimage (2:10; 12:2); one must be aggregated to those who believe (4:2), docile to the indications of the leaders (13:7, 17, 24), encouraging one's companions on the march, and taking something of their burdens on oneself (10:25, 33, 34; 12:15). To isolate oneself, to turn away from the solidarity of the group (10:25), would be to risk going astray (2:1; 13:9) and perishing; d) finally, victory belongs to those who endure and persevere, who keep going to the end.'[1]

As Christians we belong to the Church. And the Church is the People of God making its way through history to the Jerusalem above. 'Like a stranger in a foreign land,' says St Augustine, 'she presses forward amid the persecutions of the world and the consolations of God.'[2] Our own brief lives here below are taken up into that of the pilgrim Church.

In this journey, we are not left unguided or unnourished. Under the Holy Spirit, Christ instituted an ecclesiastical hierarchy with the mission of guiding and feeding the people of God in his name and gave it the authority so to do.

In the Roman Office's intercessions for Lauds of the Common of Pastors come these prayers: 'Christ our Lord, in the holy pastors you reveal your love for us; – may we never be deprived of the care you show through them. R/ Lord, nourish the lives of your people.'

'Through your sacred ministers you are present in our midst as the shepherd of our souls; – never cease to guide us through their teaching and encouragement. R/ Lord, nourish the lives of your people.'

The following is an attempt to find this nourishment. It's an exercise in listening, hoping to catch what St Augustine calls the 'one voice' of the one Shepherd speaking through the many. For clearly, over the last fifty years, the pastors of the Church have been exceptionally vocal and active, and the whole Church, sheep and shepherds, has gone through a sea-change which, in its breadth and depth, invites comparisons with other great periods of transition in Church history: the sixteenth century, the eleventh, the eighth, the fourth, the first. Through the renewal of the Liturgy no practising Catholic has been left untouched. Rather than expatiating on this, let me just acknowledge it – it seems suitably incontrovertible – and then highlight the considerable, unprecedentedly considerable, body of teaching at its heart. I mean what is found in the sixteen documents of Vatican II, in the *Catechism of the Catholic Church*, in the stream of papal encyclicals, exhortations, letters and so forth, in the documents of Roman Congregations, in the documents of Synods of Bishops and other assemblies or conferences of Bishops, and indirectly in the new liturgical books and codes of law. John Paul II alone produced fourteen encyclicals, fifteen Apostolic Exhortations, eleven Apostolic Constitutions, forty-five Apostolic Letters, gave catecheses at the General Audiences, made speeches in every part of the world, promulgated the *Catechism* and as a 'private doctor' published several books. All in all it constitutes some corpus.

The question is, what does it mean? John Paul's successor has indicated that he intends to publish less. That itself is a call to pause and reflect on this legacy. Simply too as a historical phenomenon, this material is real and interesting enough, at least if one's interested in the contemporary state of religion. Is it all, as some might say, a hopelessly rearguard action on the part of an ever less relevant Church? Terminal verbosity? Or is it, as some others allege, the symptom of an apostasy from the crystalline clarities of the past? A surrender to the spirit of the age? Again, is it just a human construct or is there a breath of the Spirit in it? Does it come from Babel or from Pentecost? No doubt often with justice, journalists, historians, critical theologians will be quick to point out the currents and counter-currents within this ocean of words, the evidence of opposing parties, the unresolved tensions, incoherences, compromises, even contradictions, the shifts of emphasis, the re-interpretations, the matters left in the shade, the unfinished business. And yet another, more sympathetic, more organic approach is also possible. Might it not be valid too, and arguably more valuable, to discern the hand of Providence in all this, to sense the leading of the one great Shepherd of the sheep, to catch in it that Shepherd's 'one voice'? And if so to find for us – simple sheep – help for our journey through the wilderness to the heavenly City, help for our life and our prayer?

Let me offer a view – personal, but I hope not hopelessly subjective.

By way of approach, it's perhaps useful to go back to another, even more authoritative if more compact, body of Christian literature, the New Testament, and especially to the Letters in it. When the Apostles or apostolic men wrote, when the author of the Letter wrote to the Hebrews or St Paul wrote to the Corinthians, why did they do so? To guide and sustain with revealed Truth a particular group of Christians in their particular situation. Why, 1,900 years later, have the successors of the Apostles and especially of Peter indulged in this immense effort? 'By means of this Council,' said Bl. John XXIII, in his address at the opening of Vatican II, '[the Church's] teaching authority, taking stock of the errors, the needs and the golden opportunities of our time, will be displayed in an extraordinary way to the whole world.' Laying aside the temptation to cynicism, *de facto* there has been an 'extraordinary display', and since the Council as well as during it. So why? In the end for the same reason as gave birth to the New Testament: to guide and encourage the members of the Church in their Christian life at a particular juncture of history by drawing on the riches of Revelation found in Scripture and Tradition. The Council and its follow-ups have been acts of the Magisterium, assisted by the Holy Spirit, not so much to put down specific heresies as to address the complex question, what does it mean to be a believer, a Christian, a Catholic, what does it mean to be the Church of Christ, at this moment / these moments of history? Remember the famous opening of *Gaudium et Spes*: 'The joy and hope, the grief and anguish of the men and women of our times ...' the last phrase in Latin being *huius temporis*. It is the sense of *hoc tempus* that has prompted the successors of the Apostles to do what they have done, to do what Peter and Paul, James and John would have done: to guide and sustain the churches of God in their Christian life. Man lives in time, in history. And if man, therefore the Christian, therefore the Church.

The joy and hope, the grief and anguish of the men and women of our time, especially of those who are poor or afflicted in any way, are the joy and hope, the grief and anguish of the followers of Christ as well, and there is nothing genuinely human which does not find an echo in their hearts. For theirs is a community made up of men and women who, united in Christ are guided by the Holy Spirit in their pilgrimage towards the Father's kingdom and are bearers of a message intended for all. This is why this community feels itself truly and deeply bound to the human race and its history (GS 1; cf. ES 26).

There has been, in Jacques Maritain's terms, an 'acceleration of history', inevitably repercussing within the life of Christians and the Church. The wealth of teaching and pastoral action that has come our way is then, to take it at its most general, an attempt to guide and stimulate, to 'renew', in the following of Christ the whole Church and each member of it, and even other Christians and any of good will prepared to listen, and this by applying revealed truth. Amid the shadows and ambiguities of any human enterprise, there is a nobility here. It should be saluted.

Now we come to the content, and the real challenge. Is it possible to synthesize in some way this great mass of material? I suggest it is, under three heads or, since my focus is the practical bearing all this has on our lives, as three imperatives.

I

As therefore you have received Christ Jesus the Lord, continue to live your lives in him, rooted and built up in him and established in the faith, just as you were taught, abounding in thanksgiving (Col 2:6–7).

So first, return to the sources! Be rooted in those things that will give you life! Draw life from them! In the rush of change that swept through the Church in the Sixties and Seventies, this was the aspect that was most easily forgotten. I think this Pope, being a quiet man, learned, elderly and contemplative, is eager to redress the imbalance. The documents that come to mind are such as *Dei Verbum* (the Dogmatic Constitution on Divine Revelation), *Sacrosanctum Concilium* (the Constitution on the Sacred Liturgy) and, derivatively, all the revised liturgical books of the Roman rite, the *Catechism of the Catholic Church*, the Trinitarian triptych of John Paul II, *Redemptor Hominis, Dives in Misericordia, Dominum et Vivificantem*, some portions of the Apostolic Letter *Novo Millennio Ineunte*, the Letter *Rosarium Virginis Mariae*, and his final encyclical *Ecclesia de Eucharistia*. The present Holy Father's *Deus Caritas Est* belongs here, as does his decision that the next Synod of Bishops take as its topic the Word of God, thus coming full circle with *Dei Verbum* which has been 'too neglected', said the 1985 Synod (*Final Relatio*).

Return to the sources! What, in the light of the above, does this mean? It means be rooted, above all, in faith and, therefore, *the* Faith. It means, understand this faith as the revelation of God's love for the world manifested in the paschal mystery of Christ and communicated to humanity by the Holy Spirit. Be centred on Christ, therefore, seeing him, man's Redeemer, always in a Trinitarian light. It means be grounded in the Word of God, transmitted by Tradition, Scripture and the Magisterium, and so, especially, read the Bible, know it, love it, eat it. It means draw life from the Liturgy, the Sacraments, and most especially the celebration of the Eucharist, which can be prolonged in adoration. It means recognize personally, whatever your place in the Church, the universal call to holiness (LG V), that is the call to belong wholly to the Lord, and at the same time develop a deeper sense of your particular vocation in the Church. It means, if you are religious, return 'to the primitive inspiration of the institute', to 'the spirit and aims of [the] founder' (PC 2).

In all of this, there is a real call not to get lost in devotional or practical or theological by-ways, but to be focused on the essential, to re-centre our Christianity on what is at the heart of it and is the best of it, to go to the pure springs for water. There is a call to put being before doing, contemplation before action (NMI 15), to cultivate what Paul VI called 'the best type of spirituality' (ES 38).

II

Now you are the body of Christ, and individually members of it (1 Cor 12:27).

The second call is: live in communion! That is, in the Church. Be ecclesial! 'Church, what do you say of yourself?' was the question the Council put to herself, especially in *Lumen Gentium*, and the mystery of the Church, her 'origin, nature, mission and destiny' (ES 9) was the central subject matter of Vatican II. Other Councils have considered the Trinity, the person of Christ, the Sacraments, faith, etc. Vatican II, completing Vatican I, focused on the Church, in both her divine and human aspects. And so a whole vision of the Church has been unrolled before the eyes of faith. It is found in the Council itself, with *Lumen Gentium* as the hub. It is found again in the *Catechism* and again in the Apostolic Exhortations on the different states of life in the Church following the Synods of 1980 on the Family, 1987 on the Lay Faithful, 1990 on the formation of priests, 1994 on the Conse-crated Life, 2000 on the Episcopate. It also surfaced in various documents of the Congregation of the Doctrine of the Faith.

The Church, in this perspective, springs from the will and action of the three Persons of the Holy Trinity. She is 'a people brought into unity from the unity of the Father, the Son and the Holy Spirit' (LG 4). She spans history and is its hidden meaning. She 'was prefigured already at the world's beginning, was prepared in marvellous fashion in the history of the people of God and the Old Covenant, was established in these last times, made manifest by the outpouring of the Holy Spirit and will be brought to glorious completion at the end of time' (LG 2). 'Constituted and organized as a society in this present world, she subsists in the Catholic Church, which is governed by the successor of Peter and the bishops in communion with him' (LG 8), 'a society structured with hierarchical organs and the mystical body of Christ, a visible society and a spiritual community, an earthly Church and a Church endowed with heavenly riches' (LG 8). She is 'essentially both human and divine, visible but endowed with invisible realities, zealous in action and dedicated to contemplation, present in the world but as a pilgrim, and so constituted that in her the human is directed toward and subordinated to the divine, the visible to the invisible, action to contemplation, and this present world to that city yet to come, the object of our quest' (SC 2). She is both the effect and the means of Christ's redemption. She is 'in Christ in the nature of a sacrament, a sign and instrument that is, of communion with God and of unity among all men' (LG 1), 'the universal sacrament of salvation' (LG 48). She is the People of God *en route* through history, the Body of Christ finding her supreme self-expression and sustenance in the Eucharist (EDE), and the Temple of the Holy Spirit which he fills with his charisms and gifts (*Catechism*). She is one, holy, catholic and apostolic. She consists of sacred ministers and lay faithful, with the consecrated life, and martyrdom above all, giving special expression to the perfection of love to which all are called (LG III-VI). She is the communion of saints, embracing the living and the dead, and always intent on the final consummation in the kingdom of the Father (LG VII), looking in her pilgrimage of faith (RM) to Mary, the immaculate mother of Christ assumed into heaven and seeing in her her own beauty and destiny summed up in one humble, glorified person (LG VIII).

'The ecclesiology of communion is the central and fundamental idea of the Council's documents,' said the 1985 Synod (*Final Relatio* II, C, 1).

So, the heart of the message appears to be that the Church is the place where God and man meet, and where the human conflict between individualism and collectivism is transcended. It is where the individual, precisely by sharing in the life of the whole, discovers both his own unique gifts and his full stature as a free human being. If each state of life in the Church has been given unprecedented attention, it is always within the horizon and for the building up of the whole, and if, in turn, the common dignity has been underlined it is not to the detriment of variety of function. As so often, what is said to religious sums it up. On the one hand, 'It is for the good of the Church that institutes have their own proper characters and functions': so, be yourself! On the other, 'All institutes should share in the life of the Church': live in communion! (PC 2b, c).

It is one of the bitterest ironies that, in the West anyway, this great effort to encourage a sense of the Church has coincided with a huge alienation from and disaffection with her (cf. 1985 Synod, *Final Relatio* I, 3).

III

To me, though I am the very least of all the saints, this grace was given, to preach to the Gentiles the unsearchable riches of Christ, and to make all men see what is the plan of the mystery hidden for ages in God who created all things (Eph 3:8–9).

So thirdly, resume the mission! Witness to charity, universally!

This flows from what goes before. It is the message that emerges from *Gaudium et Spes*, from *Ad Gentes* (the Decree on the Missionary Activity of the Church), Paul VI's *Evangelii nuntiandi* and the encyclical *Redemptoris Missio*, from *Apostolicam Actuositatem* (the Decree on the Apostolate of the Laity), but also from all that has been said on ecumenism, on non-Christian religions and, in part, on religious freedom. The social encyclicals come in here too, and the *Compendium of the Social Doctrine of the Church*, published in 2004. *Deus Caritas Est* also re-appears here.

This is a complex area. When the connection with the return to the sources and life in communion is weak, things can go flaky here. In reality, though, it is a matter of the Church looking beyond herself, to the fulfilment of God's plan to recapitulate everything in Christ. It is a matter of the Church turning to *man*, humanity as a whole in its various societies and cultures, and each individual as a whole, in order to bring it / him, redeemed, to full stature in Christ. It is a matter of the charity of Christ 'urging' us (2 Cor 5:14).

The circles are many. There is evangelization and mission in the strict sense, embracing all the efforts to spread the Gospel and found new Christian communities. There is the effort to be in dialogue with the various cultures in which the Church finds herself, to introduce the Christian leaven, to promote the true and the good in social, economic, political, international life, to contribute to a 'civilization of love'. The whole social teaching of the Church comes in here. There is the Church's educational, medical, charitable work, her 'option for the poor'. There is ecumenism, that is, the effort towards the re-establishment of the full visible unity of Christians, and beyond it inter-faith dialogue, especially with the Jews and Muslims.

Of course, there are different competencies here – the roles of the laity, the clergy, religious have to be distinguished – but everyone is implicated, and the effort is in essence a common one at the service of one divine plan.

A theology of creation is foundational here, a sense of 'man' – and the drama of his freedom – is centre-stage, and the ultimate horizon is salvific, eschatological, doxological. 'Thus the Church prays and likewise works so that into the People of God, the Body of Christ and the Temple of the Holy Spirit, may pass the fullness of the whole world, and that in Christ, the head of all things, all honour and glory may be rendered to the Creator, the Father of the universe' (LG 17).

Return to the sources, live in communion, resume the mission. I just offer that as one way of bringing together all that the Church has been offering us, over the last half-century, in the way of teaching.

'God has appointed in the church first apostles, second prophets, third teachers' (1 Cor 12:28). In our journey through the consolations and persecutions *huius temporis*, it is not simply the successors of the Apostles who guide us. Christ also acts, with the Spirit, through the saints and martyrs of our time, the founders and foundresses, the hidden holy people often very near at hand, and through the thinkers, the philosophers, the theologians. But 'first apostles ...' The Magisterium has a role. And it seems a pity if Catholics, especially educated ones, especially religious and priests, either disregard it as irrelevant to themselves or dismiss it as *a priori* suspect.

In what is on offer, three mysteries seem to be claiming us: the mystery of God, the mystery of the Church, the mystery of man. The hope is that these three become one: that the Church makes her home evermore in God, and man evermore his home in the Church of God. A beginning is that they live together in our hearts.

One last thought. We know how much for the Greek Orthodox the Holy Mountain of Athos, home of the monastic life, is an icon, distillation, concentration of the Church as a whole. And this is true of the consecrated life as such, not just in the Orthodox psyche. It is a Catholic truth. The condition of the religious life, at any moment of the Church's history, reflects – is the barometer of – the spiritual condition of the Church as a whole, or of a particular area of the Church.

Vita Consecrata, like my own little summary, falls into three parts: *confessio Trinitatis*: praise of the Trinity; *signum fraternitatis*: the sign of brotherhood; *servitium caritatis*: the service of charity. The call on the consecrated life is: i) to root itself in Christ and the Trinity; ii) to cultivate brotherhood, communion, both within the walls of each community or institute and more widely; and, finally, iii) to give itself, with renewed fervour, to charity, to mission. *Ecco!*

What the teaching Church is saying to the consecrated, therefore, summarizes, recapitulates what is being said to the whole Church.

And perhaps there's even a Benedictine twist to it. Stability, *conversatio*, obedience. In enlarged senses, the whole Church is being called to live these vows: i) to be stable, rooted in the faith, in Christ, in the Word, in the liturgy; ii) to practise *conversatio*, that is, according to the literal sense of the word, to walk, live with others, in communion, in the coenobium of the Church; iii) to be obedient, that is to make one's own again the mission Christ has received from the Father and passes on to the Church in the Spirit.

'What does it mean to be a believer, a Christian, a Catholic, what does it mean to be the Church of Christ *in hoc tempore*?' We are not left entirely without an answer. 'Christ then,' says St. Augustine,

> feeds you with judgement ... 'Those who are my sheep,' he says, 'hear my voice and follow me.' Here I find all good shepherds in the one shepherd. Good shepherds are not lacking, but they are in the one ... Away with the notion that good shepherds are lacking at present; let us not entertain the idea; may the Lord's mercy never fail to produce and appoint them. Surely if there are good sheep, there are good shepherds too, for good shepherds are made from good sheep. But all good shepherds are in the one, are all one reality. Let them feed the sheep – it is Christ who feeds them ... So he, the one shepherd, feeds his sheep in these shepherds, and they in the one ... All should speak in him with the one voice, and not with different voices ... Let the sheep hear this voice, cleared of all division and cleansed of all heresy, and let them follow their shepherd as he says, 'Those who are my sheep hear my voice and follow me.'[3]

Notes

1. Ceslau Spicq, *L'Épître aux Hébreux* (Eds du Cerf, Paris, 1950), pp. 36–7.
2. St Augustine, *City of God*, XVIII, 51, 2.
3. St Augustine, Sermon 46.29–30.

5

The Christian Way

The Christian way is different from the way of the world. So said Christ.

> The Christian way is different: harder, and easier. Christ says, 'Give me All. I don't want so much of your time and so much of your money and so much of your work: I want You. I have not come to torment your natural self, but to kill it. No half-measures are any good. I don't want to cut off a branch here and a branch there, I want to have the whole tree down. I don't want to drill the tooth, or crown it, or stop it, but to have it out. Hand over the whole natural self, all the desires which you think innocent as well as the ones you think wicked – the whole outfit. I will give you a new self instead. In fact, I will give you Myself: my own will shall become yours.'
>
> Both harder and easier than what we are all trying to do. You have noticed, I expect, that Christ himself sometimes describes the Christian way as very hard, sometimes as very easy. He says, 'Take up your Cross' – in other words, it is like going to be beaten today in a concentration camp. Next minute he says, 'My yoke is easy and my burden light.' He means both. And one can just see why both are true.

So writes C. S. Lewis in *Mere Christianity*.[1] What he says is true. There is a way of looking for happiness, the world's way, the way that comes 'naturally' to us, and there is Christ's way. And time is given us for making the journey from one to the other.

St Benedict's teaching on the renunciation of one's will –

the foundation of the whole monastic enterprise – is his equiv-
alent. 'To you my words are now addressed, whoever you
may be who, renouncing your own will to fight for the true
king Christ the Lord, take up the strong and shining weapons
of obedience' (*Rule*, Prol. 3). 'The second step of humility is
that a monk does not love his own will or delight in the satisfaction of his desires. Rather he imitates by his deeds the
Lord's saying: "I have come not to do my own will, but the
will of him who sent me"' (*Rule* 7.31–2) – 'for monks should
not have even their bodies and will at their own disposal', or,
literally, 'in their own will' (*Rule* 33.4).

Both St Benedict and C. S. Lewis point to the meaning of
following Christ. This is the famous cost of discipleship,
costing not less than everything. 'He who finds his life will
lose it, and he who loses his life for my sake will find it' (Mt
10:39). 'If any man would come after me, let him deny
himself and take up his cross and follow me' (Mt 16:24).
'Truly, truly I say to you, unless a grain of wheat falls into
the earth and dies, it remains alone; but if it dies, it bears
much fruit. He who loves his life loses it, and he who hates
his life in this world will keep it for eternal life' (Jn 12:24–5).
Our Lord does demand everything: root and branch, lock,
stock, and barrel. The Holy Spirit hands on to us the Son's
own surrender to the Father, 'so that the love with which you
have loved me may be in them, and I in them' (Jn 17:26).

I think of the wartime experiences of my parents' generation.
In a secular way – if 'secular' is the word – so many were
compelled to learn and live this truth. World War II was total
war and total war led to a quantum leap in the power of the
State to make demands upon its citizens, women as well as
men. So conscription, for example (as already in World War
I), rationing of food and fuel, restrictions on information,
movement, and so on. What was happening as deliberate
ideology in the totalitarian regimes happened from the need to
survive in the democratic regimes. The ordinary citizen had to
renounce his or her own 'will', own life-project, and hand
himself over fully to the common good of his country as

discerned by the State. If he was a young adult, he had to be prepared to lay down his life. My own father, and every uncle and aunt, in fact, did that by enlisting in the forces. Revealingly, for so many, for all the hardship and even terror, life was never again to be so rich and thrilling. 'He who loses his life will find it.' It would of course be naïve to say that all experienced it in that way – people were longing for the whole wretched thing to be over. Evelyn Waugh captured inimitably much of the petty chaos and tedium of it all. Still, I can remember an uncle telling me that the day of the D-Day landings was the high point of his life. And, surely, for many the return to tenements or suburbia was nothing but a return to the dreary and the drab, with only memories of the War serving to put sparkle or tonic into the flat water of daily life.

Our Lord in any case does know the truth about us, and if he does ask everything it's not from any perverse divine thirst for human blood. It's because he knows us. It's because nothing else will make us happy. It's because he is the one who leads creation to the achievement of its purpose. After the formation of our universe and then of our earth, after the origins of life, after the consciousness of higher forms of life, comes the emergence of the astonishing self-consciousness and capacity for self-determination of the human being. And with that a new thing enters the universe, at least potentially 'a totally new reality is enacted, one which transcends all circumstances of time, yet which itself gives point to the whole line of time. This new reality is the act of self-sacrifice deliberately carried out on behalf of others by a self-conscious being. Neither man nor God can go any further than that: there is no further to go; it is the ultimate.'[2] And ultimately, it is Christ, the God-become-man, who perfectly accomplishes this ultimate act and returns to us the capacity to do the same we had lost by the abuse of our freedom. So, 'Holiness is not an optional extra to the process of creation, but rather the whole point of it.'[3] It is even inscribed in the nature of God: 'self-surrender is ultimate; it is the ultimate in God the Father, in the Son and in the Spirit, and it is the ultimate in man, too, when he has reached the end of his crazy path.'[4] We are made to surrender. We are made to love. 'If man is the only creature on earth that God has wanted for its own sake, man can fully discover his true self only in a sincere giving of himself.'[5] The whole question – the task of the mind to discover, the choice before the will – is whom and what to love, to whom and to what to give ourselves. 'Tell me what you love and I will tell you what you are' (St Augustine).

Here is the transition before us: from the ordinary way of seeking happiness to the other way, Christ's way, the mystical way in which we are 'led by the Spirit of God' (Rom 8:14). As someone said, in the end we are either mystics or hypocrites. Either mystics or alone and sad: 'I live in loneliness, buried in ice,' wrote Max Scheler to his ex-wife in 1926. Human nature, though, our baptism, profession, every Holy Communion, experience of life all edge us the good way. All that's asked is our agreement. With grace, and the acceptance of suffering, and time, the capacity to surrender gently enlarges. The ice floes can melt into running water. What else is there for them to do?

C. S. Lewis says this too, which may be helpful:

> The real problem of the Christian life comes where people do not usually look for it. It comes the very moment you wake up each morning. All your wishes and hopes for the day rush at you like wild animals. And the first job each morning consists simply in shoving them all back; and listening to that other voice, taking that other point of view, letting the other larger, stronger, quieter life come flowing in. And so on, all day. Standing back from all your natural fussings and fittings; coming in out of the wind.[6]

We live our surrender out in the midst of our own moral messiness and that of others. We live it out in daily life. And daily life, for all the untidiness, can become a dance before the Lord. It's a question of balancing our many obligations – discerning what is to be yielded to here and now, what refused for now but kept for later – keeping each and all of them in mind and never allowing one in particular to obsess us and obscure the others. 'Be patient in tribulation, be constant in prayer' (Rom 12:12), and the Holy Spirit will draw his music out of the mess. We won't hear it perhaps, but the angels will, and we *will* be able to say, in that lovely sentence of the Letter attributed to Barnabas: 'on my pilgrimage towards holiness I have had the companionship of the Lord' (chapter 1).[7]

What a vivid sense of the beauty of the Christian way the early Christians had. Think of the Letters of Ignatius, of Clement of Rome. And Barnabas' Letter has it too. To end with his description of the Way of Light:

> Practise singleness of heart, and a richness of the spirit . . . love your neighbour more than your own life . . . whatever experience comes your way, accept it as a blessing . . . give your neighbour a share of all you have, and do not call anything your own. If you and he participate together in things immortal, how much more so in things that are mortal? . . . Do not be one of those who stretch out their hands to take but draw back when the time comes for giving . . . Day and night keep the day of judgement in mind . . . Never hesitate to give, and when you are giving, do it without grumbling; you will soon find out who can be generous with his rewards . . . And make confession of your own faults; you are not to come to prayer with a bad conscience. This is the way of Light.[8]

Notes

1. C. S. Lewis, *Mere Christianity* (Fount Pbk, London, 1977), pp. 163–5.
2. Donald Nicholl, *Holiness* (DLT, London, 1981), p. 18.
3. Ibid., p. 17.
4. H. U. von Balthasar, *Theodrama* V: *The Last Act* (Ignatius Press, San Francisco, 1998), p. 188.
5. *Gaudium et Spes*, 24.
6. Lewis, p. 166.
7. *Epistle of Barnabas*, 1.
8. Ibid., 19.

6

Homily for the Solemn Profession of Br Daniel

3 July 2003

Today, Br Daniel, in the presence of family and friends and your brethren and the saints, you are making your solemn profession as a monk. You will be consecrated as a monk forever. Had someone said to you twenty years ago, ten years even, that this is what you'd be doing in July 2003, I can imagine you giving them one of your wide-eyed, sceptical looks. But it is a pattern. Abraham and Sarah looking forward to a quiet retirement in the suburbs of Haran when the summons came. Thomas the Apostle – well, we don't know his past – but if it's true he ended in India, he must have looked back sometimes in bemusement. He had never expected his Lord and his God to be a Galilean with two legs, and a risen man with five wounds. He hadn't thought one person could mean so much, make such a difference. Life is surprising. Abraham inscribed a great circle from one tip of the Fertile Crescent to the other. St Thomas went from the shores of the Mediterranean to those of the Indian Ocean. And, under the same Providence, serving the same Mystery, obeying the same imperative, you, Br Daniel, have made your way in turn from the suburbs of London to the meadows of Moray via the goats and olives of Greece. Abraham was old when it all began, St Thomas young, and you, shall we say, in the middle – but all under the same Providence and to the same end: 'You, too,' says St Paul to the Christians of Ephesus, 'you too are being built into a house, where God lives in the Spirit.' It isn't, it can't be, a selfish exercise. Abraham became a father despite his wife's age, Thomas begot churches. As Abbot Aelred Carlyle wrote ninety years ago: 'It is not primarily for his own sake that a man is called to the life of contemplation; but it is to be dedicated to the service of prayer and penance ... a power to overcome evil and to draw fresh life and strength from the Spirit of God for the support and growth of His kingdom.' From profession onwards, on Mt Athos, every monk, ordained or not, is called father, a giver of life. Abram becomes Abraham.

What is it, Br Daniel, you're professing, vowing, today? Three things, one thing. Three things: stability, conversion of life and obedience. One thing, one quest: 'Of you my heart has spoken: "Seek his face." It is your face, O Lord, that I seek; hide not your face' (Ps 26:8-9). Three things. Stability first. It's a promise to belong, to be 'part of a building', 'part of God's household', part of this band of brothers that has had its own journey from late Victorian London dockland and a Welsh island into the Catholic Church, then on to the Cotswolds, and from there a hiving up to here; here with its own monastic past. Stability's a promise to be rooted – here, like the tree beside the waters, like the Jew in the Law, like every Christian in faith. It's a promise to stick it out, like a soldier on campaign, and with God's help to be there at the end. Conversion of life, second. It's the promise to keep inwardly moving like Abraham in response to the Word, to take up the cross daily, to let God keep building you, to grow like the tree. And obedience. 'So Abram went as the Lord told him.'

We accept a community and we accept the superior the community chooses and the Church approves. The bush, the tree let themselves be trained; the purpose is flowers and fruit. Stability the rooting, conversion the growing, obedience the fruitfulness. You're a gardener, Br Daniel; it's a great way in to spiritual things. 'I will bless you,' says the Lord – every gardener knows the need of blessing – and we will pray in the prayer of solemn blessing over you: 'Grant that our brother may live by faith, rooted in hope, always ready to receive your love and to show it to others.' Three things promised: stability, conversion of life, and obedience. Three things in view of one thing. The monk renounces mobility in order to concentrate on another journey. He renounces marriage for what marriage symbolizes. He renounces fatherhood for another way of giving life. He gives up the private possession of things for the sake of another kind of treasure. He renounces the management of his own life so that the Lord can take it over. He signs a blank cheque so God can fill it in. He promises three things for the sake of one, the quest. And he promises that quest. 'Of you my heart has spoken, "Seek his face." It is your face, O Lord, that I seek; hide not your face.' The tree turns to the sun, calm and passionate all at once, steadfast, rooted, and responding in every fibre to the pull of the sun. 'Unless I see . . . unless I touch,' said St Thomas, almost despairing but still desiring. 'The doors were closed.' In a certain sense, that's what the monk does, close the doors. But only for what happened next: 'Jesus came and stood among them. "Peace be with you," he said. Then he spoke to Thomas [knowing the speech of his heart]: "Put your finger here, look here are my hands. Give me your hand; put it into my side. Doubt no longer but believe."' The sun had turned to the tree. 'Thomas replied, "My Lord and my God"'(Jn 20:25-8, JB). He saw, he touched, and he believed. The goal of the monastic life, as a Greek monk once said to us here, is the vision of the risen Christ.

So, Br Daniel, as you make the promises, take up the life and allow yourself to be taken, be a Daniel. Be a Daniel as the Fathers of the Church saw him and Christian iconography so often portrays him. Be Daniel in the lion pit (it is one image of monastic life, to be honest!), a figure of man rescued and risen, arms uplifted, constantly praying, suggesting Christ triumphant. Be Daniel as St Gregory the Great understood him, a figure of those who take the monastic way, a 'man of desires', 'seeking the sweetness of inner knowledge', the 'delights of interior nourishment', not the rich food of a king's court. Be a Daniel who knows, in St Gregory's words, that 'an inner retreat is opened to the intending soul, if outward wandering is excluded'; who willingly accepts some lateral restraints for the sake of the upward call, 'because even a tree, prevented from spreading into branches, is led to grow in height.'[1] Your family and friends, your brethren, and the saints, St John the Baptist, St Andrew and Mary the Mother of God, are with you. May you grow tall and fruitful in this place!

Note
1. St Gregory the Great, *Morals on Job*, XXX, 39.

Part II: Growing

Speaking the truth in love, we are to grow up in every way into him who is the head, into Christ (Eph 4:15).

7

Courage

Be strong and of good courage (Josh 1:6)

What do we mean by courage? According to the dictionary, it means: 1) bravery; 2) cheerfulness or resolution in coping with setbacks. Etymologically, it goes back to the Latin *cor*, heart. It would be interesting to go round the room asking, what's your first thought on hearing the word 'courage'? It might be a person. I remember an oration given at a soldier's memorial service by a fellow tank-officer. His text was from chapter 1 of Joshua: 'Be strong and of good courage.' This soldier was, certainly, a brave soldier, and in his cheerfulness and resolution in coping with the setback of cancer proved he was a brave man.

'Be strong and of good courage.' It was a good touch to evoke Joshua. Three times at the beginning of the book of Joshua that refrain comes. Joshua, the Judges, Saul, Jonathan, David. If we were thinking biblically, it might be those figures who come to mind, or the longer litany of larger-than-life heroes of faith in chapter 11 of Hebrews. Closer to home, I remember a psychiatrist remarking that what amazed him continually was the courage of ordinary people in the face of their afflictions.

Revisiting a Virtue

It's possible, of course, either to overrate or underrate courage. Certain cultures, often cultures of particular classes, have had a cult of courage – very often courage in war, military prowess. One might think of Sparta or the Vikings or the Ottoman Janissaries or certain strata in nineteenth-century European societies, or the notorious machismo of Latin cultures. And what of ourselves?

> In the course of the last three centuries of generally advancing tameness, the British deliberately and calculatedly kept alive and nurtured a primeval, male, barbarous streak in all classes as being best suited to the armed services, buccaneering and industrial-imperial life in general . . . Whenever I witness rampaging louts, glass-smashing yobs, vomiting football crowds, my heart swells with native British pride. We are not militarist, but we are warlike.[1]

The author of those delightful sentences, by the way, is a Benedictine old boy trying to understand the ethos of his school! Our own contemporary attitudes – lager-louts aside – are harder to specify. Courage is admired, certainly, but not much taught or advocated; it is not prominent. Emphasis falls more on removing life's difficulties by social strategies or technological refinements than on meeting them with courage. The mechanical solution is always preferred to the moral: condoms to chastity.

To my mind, we need Christ to get all this right, to be truly courageous and to avoid either excess or defect in the cultivation of courage. We need his grace to be courageous, to exercise this 'virtue'. Let's begin with courage as virtue. It's the first Christian perspective on the matter. Courage, in the Christian pattern, is surely a virtue of the second-rank, an ancillary virtue, if you like, and yet at the same time thoroughly necessary, 'cardinal', pivotal. Faith, hope and charity (charity supremely) hold the first place. And so courage would be relative to them. And if one follows the usual classification of the cardinal virtues, 'fortitude', to use the Latinate name, comes only after prudence and justice, and so needs to be regulated by them, to be at their service and not vice versa. Imprudent courage is not true courage, but recklessness, bravado. Unjust courage would be mere aggression, I presume. Courage needs to find its right place. It needs 'minding'. No virtue can be healthy on its own, as a hermit. Every virtue needs the others, needs to live 'in community'. On the other hand, courage, as one of the four 'cardinal' virtues, enters into every aspect of the life of faith, hope and charity. Courage is a very useful member of the soul's community. It is impossible to be a believing, hoping and loving person without the admixture of courage. It is impossible to be a prudent, just and temperate person without at the same time being courageous. That triple exhortation to Joshua on the brink of the Holy Land has real point. Entering into the Land means entering into the promises of God, into eternal life, into the fullness of human and Christian life. To do that we need courage. I'm not sure that current Christian spirituality lays much stress on courage or fortitude. I've never heard a sermon on it. And yet how often, if we're honest, our unhappiness comes from a lack of courage before a particular situation, from moral cowardice or, in other words, because the passion of fear is mastering us rather than we it. How often are we encouraged to be 'manly'? Yet the Psalms do: 'Wait for the Lord; be strong, and let your heart take courage; wait for the Lord!' (Ps. 26:14, RSV); and again: 'Be strong and let your heart take courage, all you who wait for the Lord' (Ps 30:24, RSV). And St Paul does too: 'Be watchful, stand firm in your faith, be courageous (literally, play the man), be strong. Let all that you do be done in love' (1 Cor 16:13–14). Can the 'feminization' of spirituality go too far? 'The good thing about being a superior,' said an African prioress, delightfully emancipated from the politically correct, 'is that it makes a man of you'!

The *Catechism* says:

> Fortitude is the moral virtue that ensures firmness in difficulties and constancy in the pursuit of good. It strengthens the resolve to resist temptations and to overcome obstacles in the moral life. The virtue of fortitude enables one to conquer fear, even fear of death, and to face trials and persecutions. It disposes one even to renounce and sacrifice one's life in defence of a just cause (1808).

So the supreme example of fortitude is the martyr.

Then come two scriptural quotations: one from Psalm 117: 'The Lord is my strength and my song' (v. 14); the other from the end of the Johannine Last Discourse: 'In the world you have tribulation; but be of good cheer [or 'take courage', as the NRSV has it], I have overcome the world' (Jn 16:33).

'The Lord is my strength and my song.' Note the connection between 'strength' and 'song'. The brave person, the person in whom courage has been built in, will be a singing person, with a song in the heart. Once again, unhappiness can have to do with cowardice. And yet it's the Lord who is our strength and our song. Always in Scripture courage has its source in the Lord. How? By his providence, his presence, his grace. 'But the Lord stood by me and gave me strength to proclaim the word fully,' said St Paul (2 Tim 4:17). We stand because he stands by us. We stand because our faith, hope and love are set on him. 'We shall overcome', as they used to sing, because *he* has overcome.

Caritas forma virtutum. Every virtue comes back to love. Peter proved a coward when the Passion came. But our Lord didn't ask him afterwards, 'Simon, son of John, will you be brave next time? Will you die for me?' That was the kind of language Peter himself had used before his crash. Rather, 'Simon, do you love me?' And because his *yes* was real and a *yes* in the Lord now, he did indeed lay down his life; he was brave. Think of a mother. She will take on the whole world for the sake of her child. One is reminded of St Aelred:

> Faith is not a virtue, if it does not act through love, nor hope a virtue, if what is hoped for is not loved ... What is temperance but love which no sensual love entices? What is prudence but love which no error seduces? What is fortitude but love bravely enduring adversity? What is justice but love righting with due moderation the iniquities of this life? Charity, then, begins in faith, is exercised in the other virtues, and is perfected in itself.[2]

Courage, then, is a human virtue which in the virtuous person will have its pivotal, cardinal place. It will be a part in the whole. It will serve the whole. And in the fully mature Christian, it will be an ally and agent of his faith, hope and charity. It will enable him – to go back to the dictionary – to be 'brave', that is, actively courageous, undertaking good works for God, 'neither timorously or tardily or tepidly, nor with murmuring or the raising of objections' (*Rule* 5.14), and at the same time to be 'cheerful or resolved in facing difficulties', that is, passively courageous, 'holding fast to patience with a quiet mind and, while enduring, neither tiring nor running away'. According to St Thomas too, courage has this twofold aspect: it overcomes difficulties and endures them. Especially does it endure them, he says, surely echoing the New Testament calls to standing firm, being patient, enduring trial, and thinking of the crucified Christ. 'The principal act of courage is to endure and withstand dangers doggedly rather than to attack them.'[3] St Paul brings the two together when he says to the Thessalonians: 'We had courage in our God to declare to you the gospel of God in the face of great opposition' (1 Thess 2:2).

What the *Catechism* does in the paragraph quoted above is give a neat little sevenfold litany of that which fortitude makes possible: firmness in difficulties, constancy in the pursuit of good, the resisting of temptations and the overcoming of obstacles, the conquest of fear, the facing of trials and persecutions, readiness even to give one's life. But always 'in the Lord', in love; not of ourselves. 'In the world you will have tribulation, but take courage; I have overcome the world' (Jn 16:33).

The Gift of Courage

There is another strand, too, in the Christian tradition: fortitude as 'gift', a gift of the Holy Spirit. It is one of the spirits promised the Messiah: the spirit of counsel and might (Is 11:2), and passed on, since Pentecost, to us. 'Recall then,' writes St Ambrose to neophytes, 'that you have received the spiritual seal, the spirit of wisdom and understanding, the spirit of right judgement and courage, the spirit of knowledge and reverence, the spirit of holy fear in God's presence. Guard what you have received. God the Father has marked you with his sign; Christ the Lord has confirmed you and has placed his pledge, the Spirit, in your hearts.'[4]

This 'spirit' of fortitude is received especially in the sacrament of Confirmation. Confirmation 'gives us a special strength of the Holy Spirit to spread and defend the faith by word and action as true witnesses of Christ, to confess the name of Christ boldly, and never to be ashamed of the Cross' (*Catechism* 1303). It is an interesting fact that for a Catholic Christian to marry or be ordained or make profession, he must first be confirmed, that is, strengthened by the Holy Spirit. 'I assert that an imperfect human being needs more fortitude to pursue the way of perfection than suddenly to become a martyr,' said St Teresa. According to St Thomas, the *gift* of fortitude perfects the *virtue*, by enabling us to do things which exceed human ability. The impossible becomes possible; we are clothed with strength from on high; we act in the light of God's face and by the instinct of his Spirit; our natural trepidation is taken away and replaced by trust, confidence and security. 'I can do all things in him who strengthens me' (Phil 4:13). According also to St Thomas, Christ in Gethsemane 'first acting in the human way of the virtue of fortitude, compatible with fear, gave evidence of his trepidation . . . then immediately attained strength in the gift of fortitude.' He faced the Passion strengthened by that gift. With the same strength, the Christian can face not only the martyrdom of blood, but the white martyrdom of the ascetic life, the martyrdom of opposition and obloquy, the martyrdom of illness and old age.

Day by day

What about courage in life according to the Rule? 'Be strong and of good courage.' It's addressed to monks too. The novice needs courage. He needs it to make the necessary renunciations, to accept a new discipline, to endure the inevitable emotional turmoil. And so St Benedict says: 'If, for good reason, for the amendment of evil habit or the preservation of charity, there be some strictness of discipline, do not be at once dismayed and run away from the way of salvation, of which the entrance must needs be narrow' (Prologue 47–8). The mature and active monk needs courage. Principally the courage that ensures, in the *Catechism*'s phrase, 'constancy in the pursuit of good'. 'Day and night unceasingly' he must employ the tools of good works (*Rule* 4.76) He might prefer to be rid of some of his tasks or be pained at being passed over in areas where he feels a competence. He is unlikely not to encounter, in his obedience, some 'hard and contrary things and even injustice' (7.35), but he holds to patience and perseveres, avoiding the pitfalls of murmuring and cynicism. The ageing monk, too, needs courage, as his bodily powers and mental faculties decline. And, surely, these admonitions apply to all Christians.

'Be strong and of good courage.' It's true in a very humble, daily way. Every day we're called to enter and conquer the Land. There's a courage of the morning, of the afternoon, of the evening, and sometimes of the night as well. Courage, if we think of it, has a full day's work. She has to lead us to and through our work in the early morning. She will have to master our itchiness and keep us regular. She'll probably need to nudge us to the difficult or boring job we have put off for too long. When we start to wilt inside, she'll have to leave her contemplations and do her best to buoy us up. We fail, or we make a mistake. Courage will whisper, 'Admit it and don't shift the blame.' She'll need to steer us away from the underhand and insincere. She'll help us to frank and healthy mutual relations, and keep us cheerful. It's a long and full day for her, and she'll have suffered some wounds in the course of it. But her last words, after we've examined our consciences, will be consoling: 'Do not be frightened or dismayed, for the Lord your God is with you wherever you go' (Josh 1:9).

One last courage comes to mind. It's one the *Benedictus* reminds us of each morning: 'that we, being rescued from the hands of our enemies, might serve him without fear, in holiness and righteousness before him all our days' (Lk 1:74–5).

It's courage before the Lord. It's the courage needed to turn to the Lord, to climb the first step of humility and live the contemplative life. Whenever we turn to God, we meet ourselves. It's an anticipation of the Last Judgement. We need courage to do that. And then we need courage to move beyond ourselves and into God. Love makes us courageous, but love takes courage too. And perhaps in the end courage is simply that: the courage to love, and therefore the courage to die – for the Lord, as well as in the Lord. The courage to pray and to persevere in prayer.

Notes

1. John Martin Robinson, *Grass Seed in June* (Michael Russell, Norwich, 2006), p. 69.
2. St Aelred, *Mirror of Charity* I, 31, 89.
3. St Thomas Aquinas, *Summa Theologiae* 2-2, 123, 6.
4. St Ambrose, *De Mysteriis* 7, 42.

8

The Little Foxes

There is one thing it is essential to say: that it's worth combating small faults and failings in ourselves. Even if we fail, it is worth it. This may seem to have nothing to do with Eastertide, but it is spring and the soul is a garden. And how much of a gardener's time in spring is spent fending off pheasants and rooting out couch-grass and bishop's weed. As Baudelaire said, 'the world is a forest of symbols'. Weeds, ivy, pheasants, snakes, the 'little foxes' of the Song of Songs. One pheasant got in under the nets the other day and ate its way through practically a whole row of brassicas. And that, of course, is the great reason for being vigilant over these lesser threats. They encroach, they proliferate, overrun. Irritability, impatience, for example. It's almost as if a second personality forms itself around us – not the personality we really want, nor even the one that we really are, but still there and affecting other people's perceptions of us and all our relationships. A sort of patina is formed. And the shine is lost, the 'holy glow' that a fervent Christian can give off. In Argentina, there's a parasitical tree that can lodge in another and eventually enshroud the whole of it so that it's impossible to know what the original tree is.

Our little faults – temperamental, mainly – are left to humble us. They're left to prevent other people confusing us with Christ and therefore ceasing to live by faith. They're left, as Trent says, of concupiscence, for us to struggle with, for us to have something to do, to prove our love and our concern. They're left so that we may learn, in God's time, that it is God who makes us free and not we ourselves. They have their place in God's providence and can be turned to good in so many ways. Sometimes, we must remember the parable of the wheat and the darnel, and prefer to accentuate the good rather than beam in on the evil, spending our money on fertilizer rather than weed-killer. 'There is a time to plant and a time to pluck up.' But when we do try to pluck up, we do well – if we're calm and methodical about it. And maybe the discerning will realize we're trying, and will take courage themselves – and so good will spread.

I think the morning is important here, perhaps especially the morning *lectio*. We should try to tune in to the word of God. 'Morning by morning he wakens, he wakens my ear, to hear as those who are taught' (Is 50:4). 'O that today, you would listen to his voice, harden not your hearts' (Ps 94, RSV). Somehow if we can get on the wavelength, then there's the possibility of keeping it throughout the day, or at least of returning to it whenever we sense we've lost it. Then, for the evening perhaps, daily examination of conscience – an ancient monastic practice going back to St Antony. 'We will gain so much from this,' says John Chrysostom rather optimistically, 'that should we do it only for a month we would find ourselves fully clothed in virtue.' And sensitivity of conscience is said to be one of the great fruits of frequent confession.

Snakes I find in St Benedict (along with the *Ladder*). Words can be useful, and in the Rule there are two, almost indistinguishable and equally vivid: *subrepere* and *subripere*. Together they occur four times: in chapter 39.7: 'Above all things, gluttony must be avoided, so that a monk may never be surprised by a surfeit (indigestion), *subripiat*'; in chapter 40.5: 'Let the superior always take care that neither excess nor drunkenness creep in, *subrepat*'; in chapter 57.7: 'As regards price, let not the sin of avarice creep in, *subripiat*'; in chapter 67.4: 'Let them [returning from a journey] ask the prayers of all on account of any faults that may have surprised them on the road, by the seeing or hearing of something evil, or by idle talk, *subripuerint*.'

St Benedict uses *subripere* three times and *subrepere* once, but it is fair to say that in at least two of the occasions where *subripere* is used it has the meaning of *subrepere*. Put the two verbs together, in fact, and a vivid image emerges. *Subrepo* is made of *sub*, meaning under or beneath, and *repa* meaning creep. So it gives us: to creep forth beneath or from below; to come on unawares, insensibly, by degrees. *Subripio* is made of *sub* and *rapio*, meaning pluck, seize. So we have: to snatch or take away from below, secretly, covertly. It's impossible not to think of the serpent in the garden, first of all creeping stealthily along, insinuating its doubts into Eve's mind, and then snatching her goodness away. So, St Benedict is saying (39 and 40), gluttony works, whether in food or drink: a creeping over-preoccupation with palate and stomach, with the table, then a sudden disaster, perhaps. More generally, how easily preoccupation with personal health, personal comfort encroaches. So (57) avarice works: a creeping over-preoccupation with money can get hold of someone – nothing dishonest, hopefully, but a disorientation, a shift in priorities, hard to notice, just everything being valued for what it can 'bring in'. And behind avarice, lies work. Activism. It is extraordinary how work can take over, just like bishop's weed or ivy. How it can fill the time of prayer, for example.

So images, contacts, habits gradually take possession, become our life. The daily encounter with the newspaper means more than the daily encounter with the Bible. The arrival of the postman is the daily parousia. The visits of friends loom larger than the needs of community. Here we have the little creeping, plucking things – the couch-grass and the pheasants – that can so damage the growth, spoil the spring. The serpents in the garden. Think of the worldliness thing. We can become addictively secular, even aggressively so. And this has all happened gradually, imperceptibly, creeping up on us. And whether the serpent creeps in by way of the body or of work or of the world, what is it he's really after? Very simply: the erosion of prayer. Lose prayer and you've lost. Stick to it and you've won.

'Catch the foxes for us, the little foxes that make havoc of the vineyards, for our vineyards are in flower' (Song 2:15, JB). This is the classic text here.

Who are these nefarious foxes? First, they represent, on the historical plane, all those nasty and detested little neighbours who in their cowardice took advantage of the fact that Israel was in exile after the ruin of Jerusalem to come and loot the land and settle in a country that did not belong to them. Deuteronomy already gives a good list of them: 'the Hittites and the Amorites, the Canaanites and the Perizzites, the Hivites and the Jebusites' (20:17), and this is echoed in the Lamentations of Jeremiah: 'because Mt Zion is desolate; jackals roam to and fro on it' (Lam 5:18). But the vineyard of Yahweh Sabaoth is not only the Holy Land, it is each of our lives.[1]

And so to help torch the foxes we turn to the Fathers.

'If you take these words as referring to the soul who joins herself to the Word of God, the foxes must be understood as the opposing forces and the wicked powers of demons who by means of base thoughts and perverted notions destroy the blossom of the virtues ... and ruin the fruit of faith.' The angels come to our help here, says Origen, suggesting to us that these thoughts 'do not come from God, but from the Evil One, and imparting to the soul the power to discern the spirits'. Yes, we need the light of discernment. And catch the bad thoughts while they're young, 'for as long as a bad thought is only beginning it is easily driven from the heart. But if it comes again and again, and goes on for long, it surely leads the soul to agree with it; and, once agreed to and entrenched in the heart, it is certain to result in the commission of sin.' Understanding the Song to be a dialogue between Christ and the Church, makes the little foxes those just beginning to teach false doctrine.[2]

For Gregory of Nyssa, the little foxes are the powers of evil, 'those terrestrial powers who struggle against mankind, the principalities and powers and the cosmic rulers of darkness and the spirits of wickedness' – but all cut down to size, simply 'little foxes, pitiful and miserable when compared with our strength. If you conquer them, you will win a grace that will be your own.' And the vine, 'which is our human nature', will begin 'to put forth its clusters of fruit'. Optimistic stuff.

St Bernard, no surprise, has plenty to say. The vineyard is the wise man, the spiritual man 'within whom all things are

cultivated, all things are germinating, bearing fruit and bringing forth the spirit of salvation'.

> The Man-God loves men, not trees, and counts our progress as
> his own fruits. Unflaggingly he watches for their season, smiles
> when they appear, and anxiously strives that we should not lose
> them when they do appear; or rather that he should not lose them,
> for we are as dear to him as he is. With foresight then he orders
> that the cunning little foxes be caught for him, lest they pilfer the
> immature fruits (Sermon 63.5).

After some digression, he then turns to the foxes. They are
'temptations'. More particularly, they are the temptations of
'proficients' rather than 'beginners'. Though it's clear he has
monks in mind, and is really telling stories from experience,
his warnings might equally apply to lay Christians. Fox No.1:
the desire to evangelize one's family and friends. No.2: the
desire to evangelize anyone and everyone. No.3: the attraction
of the solitary life. No.4: singularity in asceticism. It's all
very Bernard. The point is the subtlety of this threat. These
are not the crude and obvious vices, but 'certain subtle vices
cloaked in the likeness of virtues'. Hence the epithet 'little'.
'They cannot easily be avoided except by the perfect and the
experienced, and by such as have the eyes of their souls
enlightened for the discernment of good and evil, and particularly for the discernment of spirits.' This hearkens back to
Origen. 'Catch me the little foxes,' says the text: not exter-
minate, drive away, kill, but 'catch'. In other words, discern
them, recognize them, expose them, bring them into the light
of day. That's all that's needed. 'Once recognized, it can do
no harm; if it is recognized, it is conquered' (Sermon 64.1–7).

St John of the Cross comes to the little foxes in Stanza XVI
of the *Spiritual Canticle*. 'Catch us the foxes, For our vineyard is now in flower.' The flowering vineyard is the bride,
the soul, now well-established in virtue, 'united with her
Bridegroom according to the will ... enjoying habitual peace
in the visits of her Beloved', and eager to yield to the 'interior delight of love', which is the wine the vineyard of virtue
yields. Paradoxically, it's now the troubles begin. The devil

(cf. Origen and Gregory) would 'rather hinder a small frac-
tion of this soul's rich and glorious delight than make many
others fall into numerous serious sins'. And so he stirs up
trouble at every level. Why foxes? Because, he claims, foxes
pretend to be asleep in order to catch their prey. And so all
the forces of disorder within and without us seem to be asleep,
until 'the flowers of virtue rise and blossom in the soul'. 'At
that moment, it seems that the sensual flowers of the appetites
and sense powers awaken and arise in the sensory part of the
soul in an effort to contradict the spirit and reign.' 'Many
various kinds of images are brought to the memory and phan-
tasy and many appetites and inclinations are stirred up in the
sensory part.' The flesh lusts against the spirit. And then the
demons come in to exacerbate the trouble: stimulating the
appetites, triggering the imagination, even producing physical
problems, noises, and worse 'spiritual terrors and horrors that
sometimes become a frightful torment'. And so we pray to the
angels: 'Catch us the foxes, for our vineyard is now in
flower.' It's the angels' duty to assist us by putting the devil
to flight. 'It is not in a person's power to be free of these
disturbances until the Lord sends his angel round about them
that fear him and delivers them, and until He brings peace and
tranquillity, both in the sensory and spiritual part of the soul.'

In the *Living Flame of Love*, the little foxes have another
meaning. They are the untimely operations of the soul when
it should be yielding to the draw of contemplation and stillness
(55).

In a letter of St Francis de Sales, there is a particular appli-
cation of some interest. He is writing to a monastery of Benedictine nuns in Paris. Their house is in good order, but for
some small things. Some nuns had their own pensions and
therefore got better treatment for themselves when ill; some in
good health had 'particular indulgences in food and dress
without necessity'; their conversations and recreations were
'not entirely edifying'.

> 'Catch us,' says the Canticle, 'the little foxes which destroy the
> vines.' They are little; do not wait till they become great; for if
> you wait it will not only not be easy to catch them, but by the

time you would catch them they will already have spoilt everything.

It was the failures in the vow of poverty that most disturbed him. 'One can be a good religious without reciting in choir, without wearing this or that particular habit, without abstinence from such and such things; but without poverty and community of goods no one can be so.'[3]
Thoughts from the demons, the subtler temptations of the Christian, the disturbances that fall on those entered on the way of contemplation, the little infidelities of religious. 'Catch us these.' Catch us the little faults. This is Eastertide and the light of Christ shines in it. It's a symbol of the illuminative way. And that light will include the light to see our faults, not frantically but calmly. And maybe we will find the energy of Christ rising in us like the sap is rising in the trees, and with that energy not grow weary in the spiritual combat, but chase away some pheasants, root out some weeds and catch the odd little fox.

Notes

1. Blaise Arminjon, *The Cantata of Love: a Verse by Verse Reading of the Song of Songs* (Ignatius, San Francisco, 1988).
2. Origen, *Commentary on the Song of Songs* III, 15.
3. St Francis de Sales, *Letters to Persons in Religion*. Library of St Francis de Sales, Vol. IV, tr. Canon Mackey, OSB (Burns & Oates, London, 1901), Letter 60.

9

Four Silences

The Lord is our Shepherd. He always wants to lead us deeper and further – into holiness, into his likeness. We trust that, for most of us most of the time, habitual mortal sin is not the issue. So what does conversion mean? Among the many possible answers to that question, could it be silence?

Here are three familiar texts beloved of the monastic tradition:

> It is good to wait in silence for the Lord to save (Lam 3:26).

> In returning and rest you shall be saved; in quietness and in trust shall be your strength (Is 30:15).

> While gentle silence enveloped all things, and night in its swift course was now half gone, your all-powerful word leaped from heaven, from the royal throne ... (Wis 18:14–15).

Silence, it must be said at once, is not an absolute. It's one partner in a marriage, the other being speech. St Benedict is at least as preoccupied with the right use of the word as with abstention from it. And as speech needs silence to be fruitful, so silence needs speech. It's one member of a family, one strength among many, needing the others to give of its best, needing charity especially. It's not an unequivocal good. Said Abba Poemen: 'A man may seem to be silent, but if his heart is condemning others he is babbling ceaselessly. But there may be another who talks from morning till night and yet he is truly silent; that is, he says nothing that is not profitable.'[1]

Silence heals. Modernity, and its machinery, conspire against silence, and so against the human spirit's health. Is there anywhere in our country it's impossible to hear traffic or aeroplanes? Long ago Kierkegaard said: 'The present state of the world and the whole of life is diseased. If I were a doctor and were asked for my advice, I should reply, Create silence! Bring men to silence.'[2]

Then, of course, there is the irony of talking about silence at all. 'I cannot explain silence in words,' said that wise poet, George Mackay Brown. Silence is to be heard, experienced, lived. Silence, as St Benedict says (*Rule* 6.3), has its own *gravitas*, its weight, its pull.

Silence has many forms. Let me try to touch on four of them.

There is, first of all, a tactical, practical silence (though such adjectives do not do it justice). Who, here, would have thought of Amos? But in one fierce oracle against the practitioners of injustice and oppression, he suddenly remarks: 'Therefore he who is prudent will keep silent in such a time; for it is an evil time' (5:13). This is silence in time of trial, silence when under attack, silence before sinners, evil persons, demons. This is one of the majestic silences of the biblical and Christian tradition. It is the silence of the Psalmist before his enemies in Psalm 38, stirringly commented on by St Ambrose: 'the just person is his own cloister ... the just person keeps silent in the face of insolence; the just person prays.' Was he thinking of his encounters with Arians and Emperors? It is the silence of suffering Jerusalem, laid waste by the enemy, by her own sins (Lam 3:25–30). It is the silence of the Messiah before his judges, the Sheep before his shearers, Christ in his passion (Mt 26:63). It is the silence of the martyrs in the midst of their sufferings, silence filled with prayer. It's the silence with which the Christian silences the talk, the confusion, the crashing sounds, the manic laughs of the demons. This is the counsel of the great St Antony: 'If one pays no attention to them, they cry out and lament as though vanquished ... "But I, as a deaf man, heard not; and was as a deaf man not opening his mouth. And I was as a man that hears not." So let us pay them no heed, treating them as strangers, and let us not obey them, even when they rouse us for prayer or talk to us about fasting.'[3]

It's the silence with which St Benedict's monk, in the midst of hard and difficult things and even injustices, 'embraces patience' (7.35). It's the silence which, intriguingly, the dissidents of the Soviet period rediscovered as the only weapon capable of defeating the interrogators of the NKVD and KGB. Argue, play their game, and you're lost. How agonizingly topical this silence must be for so many! One thinks of the falsely accused. It's the silence that looks for the resolution of misunderstandings, for reconciliations, answers to 'problems', healings of wounds, redressings of injustice, the revivifying of the Church and so on, not to human means, human justice, human reason, but to God and to God's great co-worker, time. Of course – it's the whole bias of contemporary wisdom – there are times when protests must be made, law invoked, the clear word spoken, arguments deployed. These things too, in their way, can be bulwarks against evil, against the demonic. 'For evil to triumph all that's needed is the silence of the good.' But still, the other, ancient wisdom holds as well. As there is a time to speak, there can be 'a time to keep silence' as well (Eccles 3:7). Often, more often perhaps than we are likely to think, silence is wisdom. 'Even though the word of God is in you, in God's word you will be silent; and in your silence you will cry out, in such a way that God will hear you.'[4] That is St Ambrose. And so is this – worth remembering if anything is – 'The devil loves noise; Christ looks for silence.'[5] 'Remember the words,' St Ambrose goes on, '"He was like a lamb before his shearer, not opening his mouth." And again: "He shall not cry out or contend; neither shall anyone hear his voice in the street, until he shall have shown forth his judgement in victory." This, of course, refers to his victory over the Serpent.' That is a first silence, then: 'the silence of victory over the Serpent'. At its heart, it is a silence of patient waiting, of trust in the Lord.

A second silence is a most mysterious one: 'the silence of the

Father'. There has never been a feast of God the Father, because Christian liturgy celebrates the revelation of the Father's love 'in the Son'. There has never been an icon of God the Father, because the icon is the Son. In the same way, St Ignatius will speak of 'Jesus Christ his Son, who is his Word proceeding from silence.'[6] The Father is silence, a silence that speaks in his Word. What a reality to let ourselves into: the eternal silence of the Father, from which the eternal Word is eternally spoken! First, there is Silence, then there's the Word. In Jewish tradition, silence precedes creation. In the Jewish day, first there is night, then day. 'And evening came, and morning came, the first day' (Gen 1:5). And so it is. In everything, there are things that are first and things that are second. In a fallen world, the latter are preferred to the former, the former live under the heel of the latter, and in our contemporary world, doubly fallen because fallen from redemption as well as creation, this is even more so. In reality, though, first there is silence, then there is the word. First there is hunger, then there is eating. First there is virginity, then there is mating. First there is place and staying in a place, then there is movement. First there's the earth and the land, then the town and the city. First there's the heart, then there's the head. First there's contemplation, prayer, reflection, then there's action. First there's worship, then there's work. First there's God, then there's man.

Prayer is the entry into this silence. 'Contemplative prayer is *silence*,' says the *Catechism*, quoting SS Isaac of Nineveh and John of the Cross, 'the "symbol of the world to come" or "silent love". Words in this kind of prayer are not speeches; they are like kindling that feeds the fire of love. In this silence, unbearable to the "outer" man, the Father speaks to us his incarnate Word, who suffered, died and rose; in this silence the Spirit of adoption enables us to share in the prayer of Jesus' (*Catechism* 2717).

Which brings us to silence in his presence. The prophets already knew this: 'But the Lord is in his holy temple; let all the earth keep silent before him' (Hab 2:20). There are similar texts in Zephaniah (1:7) and Zechariah (2:13). They all seem to invoke the Lord of the Temple, the Lord present in the Temple, the living and true God liable to burst out like a flame. What's suggested here is silence in God's presence, the silence proper to God's house, the silence that is overture and prelude to the mighty works of God. Just as Jewish tradition linked silence and creation, so it linked silence and the Temple. According to the second-century BC *Letter of Aristeas*, 700 priests functioned in the Temple in complete silence. According to other sources, the incense offering was made in silence. If so, the Gospel of Luke begins in silence (Lk 1:8ff.). Then there is that intriguing note in 1 Kings 6:7, describing the construction of Solomon's Temple: 'When the house was built, it was with stone prepared at the quarry; so that neither hammer nor axe nor any tool of iron was heard in the Temple.' Is this a more or less conscious background for St Benedict's contemporary, the Syrian Monophysite Philoxenus of Mabbug, who wrote: 'Material silence introduces us to spiritual silence, and spiritual silence lifts a man up to live in God. But if a man stops living in the company of silence, there will be no meeting with God'? And for John Climacus when he writes: 'The lover of silence draws close to God [the language of Temple liturgy]. He talks to Him in secret, and God enlightens him'?[7] In the temple of Christ's Body, the lover of silence meets the living God.

Let me develop the image a little. We ourselves are the house of God, indwelt by the Living One, present in our consciences as judgement and mercy. In a letter to the Empress Agnes, St Peter Damian alludes to the building of Solomon's Temple and says this most wonderful of things: 'When the noise of human talking comes to an end, the temple of the Holy Spirit can be built up within you by silence.' The Lord wants to share the house with us, to make it the temple of the Holy Spirit. If we open our house to him and allow him in, we will find hitherto unknown parts of us opening up, rooms we'd never looked in. This can be, sometimes, extremely painful. They may be rooms long locked, full of difficult things, and suddenly, so to speak, they are spilling into the corridors. Why does this happen? Because we have handed Christ the keys. At other times, we may have lived so superficially in our house that we didn't know these rooms were there; we didn't know of the inner chamber where our Father sees us in secret and Jesus awaits us. But now Jesus is taking possession of the house, room by room, the idols going out by the window. The Shekinah is making its rounds like a burning torch, 'search[ing] Jerusalem with lamps' (Zeph 1:12). Prophecy is being fulfilled: even 'the pots in the house of the Lord shall be as the bowls before the altar; and every pot in Jerusalem and Judah shall be sacred to the Lord of hosts ... And there shall no longer be a trader in the house of the Lord of hosts on that day' (Zech 14:20–21). The Lord is claiming and cleansing the Temple. And silence, somehow, is intrinsic to this process. 'The temple of the Holy Spirit [is] built up within you by silence.' For, beyond the bitter-sweetness of the process, over the doorway of the house it is 'Peace to this house' that has been written. His purposes are always 'peace at the last'. 'And it shall be inhabited, for there shall be no more curse; Jerusalem shall dwell in security' (Zech 14:11). And peace and silence are very close friends. The more the Lord gives peace, the more he gives silence, 'the mystery of the world to come.'[8] 'At first,' wrote Isaac of Nineveh, 'it's we who constrain ourselves to be silent. Then something is born from our silence, which attracts us to silence. May God give you grace to perceive what is born of silence.'[9]

So we come to a fourth and final silence, interior silence. What is it? Silence, surely, of the clamour of our needs. An enterprising fellow in the late 1930s calculated there were some twenty-one of these needs in the human being! Knowing the same, St Augustine said, 'It is better to need less than to have more.' It's not that needs are wrong. But it is their clamour, their capacity to obsess, their lack of reason and measure that oust the silence; their capacity to occupy that centre stage, that inner space, which is Christ's throne. The silence of interior anger, judging, criticizing. The silence of the 'thoughts', 'calm of mind, all passion spent'. The silence of worry. The silence of self-preoccupation. The silence of ambition.

'To someone who has experienced Christ himself, silence is more precious than anything else,' said Philoxenus of Mabbug again. Is there a single saint on the Church's roll who would not agree, or cherish silence? And why? Because they've experienced Christ. 'Silence is one of the most certain signs God is living in a soul,' said a nineteenth-century monk. Such fragile, inner silence as comes our way comes from the peace, the *shalom*, the fullness of the presence of Christ, the indwelling Word. It is a beautiful thing when we meet it: people whose hearts are held by silence. Jesus is its secret. 'Jesus came and stood among them and said, "Peace be with you"' (Jn 20:19). And that's where he always is: in the midst of us, and in the midst, at the heart, of each of us. There he sounds, 'a voice that speaks of peace, peace for his people and his friends and those who turn to him in their hearts' (Ps 84:9).

'God is always so close,' said a Carthusian once. 'A little bit of silence and a little bit of peace, and I could catch Him. But a little more silence and a little more peace, it's He who catches us. And that's much better' (Dom Jean-Baptiste Porion, Valsainte).

Notes

1. Søren Kierkegaard, *For Self-Examination* (Princeton Uni. Press, 1991), p. 48.
2. *Sayings of the Desert Fathers* 27 (Cistercian Publications, Kalamazoo, 1984).
3. St Athanasius, *Life of Antony* 26, 27.
4. St Ambrose, *Commentary on Psalm 38:7*.
5. St Ambrose, *Commentary on Psalm 45:11*.
6. St Ignatius, *Magnesians* 8, 2.
7. St John Climacus, *The Ladder of Divine Ascent*, Step 11.
8. St Isaac of Nineveh, *On Religious Perfection* 65.
9. Ibid.

10

Taking the Curve

The Mid-Life Crisis, St Peter and the Paschal Mystery

'He has broken my strength in mid-course' (Ps 101:24). The first thing to question, of course, is the very phrase 'mid-life crisis', especially 'crisis'. Better I think, but for its gynaecological associations, would be 'mid-life change of life'. It doesn't always entail a 'crisis' in the popular, melodramatic sense. I've no idea whether psychologists still talk of 'life-cycles', but surely our life can be seen as a series of interlocking arcs, or arches – each with its *arsis* and *thesis*. Childhood, adolescence, young adulthood, middle adulthood, senior adulthood, and then whatever it is that follows next! Each begins before the preceding one ends. So there is overlap: one arc ending, another springing up; one world dying, another struggling to be born. Hence the *potential* for crisis (but not the *inevitability*).

Anyway, sometime between the later thirties and the early fifties, there *is* a change. It can be big, as big as that between childhood and adolescence. A *physiological* change, affecting everything from the private parts to the brain, not to mention toenails and the pate! A *psychological* change, an irruption of buried memories, new perceptions, new perspectives. A 'paradigm shift'; a change of inner landscape; a new restlessness. One image would be of the old Roman chariot races. After the long straight run, or the crazy, passionate, jostling gallop of early adulthood comes the sharp, narrowing bend. It's the moment when spectacular derailing can occur, when the art of 'taking the curve' is greatly to be prized. But, once round the bend, another straight appears, taking one through as far as health permits. I wonder if what Dorothy L. Sayers once said of women doesn't apply, *mutatis mutandis*, to men as well: 'Not enough is made in biographies written about women of the dynamic effects of menopause. It often happens that the change in hormonal balance and the realignment of psychic forces result in a clarification of purpose and a heightened energy.'[1] Certainly, male or female can emerge clarified in his or her vocation, or station in life, and more at one.

So, danger, yes, but opportunity, too. Second careers, second marriages, second winds: they can be for the good, an entry into truth and life, a final disengagement from the tangles of childhood and adolescence and the mistakes that followed. A real re-birth. Many return to the Church at this time, or find their vocation within it. So, opportunity, yes. But – then again – danger, too. Plain silliness at times. Think of a woman who left her admittedly dull but undeniably decent husband, took up with a younger fellow, predictably on drugs and suitably tattooed, and, in the midst of it all, made the lid-lifting comment: 'I feel as though I'm seventeen again.' A psychiatrist once remarked of a man acting wildly: 'You must realize we're dealing with a seventeen-year-old.' The man was, of course, middle-aged. The hope must be that the physiological and psychological changes are 'ridden', are turned to good and to God, by a *spiritual* change, a second conversion, a passover of the Lord. If arches are a valid image, surely each in turn can support life's aqueduct, the stream of the Spirit through my life. Each is a gift that grace can fill.

'He has broken my strength in mid-course.' This, though, touches on something central to the process. With the forties come the intimations of mortality: the real realization that one isn't going to live for ever. The horizon is suddenly nearer. And it can be that – the fearful refusal to face it, more precisely – that triggers the ridiculous. There is a phrase in Hebrews about 'those [i.e. us, human beings] who through fear of death were subject to lifelong bondage' (Heb 2:15). The fear of death can drive to sin. A person can have a sense that somehow 'life has passed him by', that he has missed the boat. This is the 'last chance' then. It seems the central challenge of mid-life is a coming to terms with the prospect of death; for the believer, a deeper, more personal appropriation of Christ's victory over death. Robert Lowell's luminous reply to an interviewer comes back to me often: 'What is it that gets you about life?' 'That people die.' 'From the time I was forty, I've thought about death every day,' said my parish priest once. 'To keep death daily before one's eyes' is a tool for taking the curve (*Rule* 4.47). At the very least, I have to face the fact – for the first time in my life – that *I'm no longer young*. There's another, alien, pushy generation behind me. Once I'm forty, most Africans (most human beings) are younger than me.

'He has broken my strength in mid-course.' It can be literally so for some. Cancer is discovered in oneself or in a loved one; marriage ends in tears and worse; some indiscretion or change of circumstances end a career ... Monastic life, priestly ordination, are not a certificate of exemption from these or their equivalents.

From the late teens, early twenties, what is happening, what is one doing? Let's risk some generalizations, even though there'll be as many variations as individuals. Affirming oneself, essentially; taking one's role in life's play; fashioning one's own world-view, one's personal synthesis; trying to bring one's actual life into harmony with one's ideals. 'I write to you, young men, because you are strong and the word of God abides in you, and you have overcome the evil one' (1 Jn 2:14). In a way, the 'strong, young' monk is a perfect exemplar of all this. He is channelling his libido or energy or whatever towards the things of God, as he perceives them. He is getting it together. He is being generous. He is honing his will and his judgement and his actions. More and more, he knows what he thinks and what he wants. Oh! It's not impossible the river won't always keep within its banks. The drive, the thrust; the 'must know', 'must do', 'must have'; the insistence that others embrace the right thing with equal enthusiasm ... These things are not impossible ...

The time comes, though, when this curve begins imperceptibly to dip. Yes, perhaps there will be a sudden, dramatic breaking of strength in mid-course. More likely, God willing, something more gentle. Yes, somehow the energy isn't quite there any more, at least not so superabundantly. Somehow the previous sources of inspiration lose their power to fire. No more exciting prospects on the horizon, just the same old self, same old others, same old job. The hunch that the perfect soul-friend, that Samaritan to bind up all the wounds, is never actually going to come by; nor the Beatrice to my Dante, for that matter. In countless oblique and subtle ways, life signifies that it isn't entirely playing ball, isn't quite a gentleman, isn't delivering the goods. And one starts to wonder, maybe 'life' here is the angel of God.

The Greek novelist Nikos Kazantsakis once interviewed an old monk on Mt Athos. 'Do you still struggle with the devil?' he asked him. 'No,' the man replied. 'I used to, but I've grown old and tired and the devil has grown old and tired with me. Now I leave him alone and he leaves me alone!' 'So your life is easy then, no more struggles?' 'Ah no,' replied the monk, 'it's worse. Now I struggle with God!'

In this wilderness, the old temptations can come back, newly dressed, or new ones suddenly spring up from the ground. Heart-wrenching yearnings for attention and affection; aching loneliness; new depths of anger perhaps; or just plain *taedium vitae*, middle-aged acedia; disillusionment, with the Church, the world, family, colleagues; loss of faith, loss of hope ... 'Why this waste?' (Mt 26:8), as Judas said. And so the temptation to look for 'let-outs': the compensations of hyperactivity, authority, projects, relationships. Or, conversely, the insistence that everyone focus on my crisis. Anything to get out of the desert ...

If I paint the picture in sombre hues, it's only to light up, I hope, the forward path. While one arch is falling, another is rising, and it's the outlines of that I want to trace. Many others' wisdom has touched on this from different angles;[2] they've each got something to offer. So has Jean Vanier, of course. He will say middle life is the time for accepting the wound, realizing it's inherent, walking with it rather than running from it, recognizing that in a mysterious way the Holy Spirit is at the centre of it.[3] Acceptance is central. He also says somewhere, 'What God asks of the middle-aged is fidelity.'

I am always more than my situation. *I* go through a difficult period, *I* am middle-aged. I'm *not* my difficulty. I'm *not*
simply my age. I'm always other and more. It's the difference
between 'being' and 'having', substance and accident. I can
never be simply identified with whatever I'm enduring,
however absorbing. The way out and on is precisely uncover-
ing that more. With God's grace, I like to think, what can
happen is that the best of each stage, each arch of the aqueduct is carried over into the next, and thereby never lost. The
childlikeness, not the childishness; the idealism of youth, not
the moodiness; the purposefulness and clarity of younger
manhood, not the arrogance and ambiguity. And so on. None
of the good things should disappear. Each stage simply re-
positions the previous one. The person who has gone through
the mid-life change needn't lose the drive, the holy ambitions
of his earlier years. But he has been changed, been marked.
And there's something inside him now he knows is worth infinitely more than all his own ideas and desires. They are all
quite secondary.

My own offering, for what it's worth, is St Peter. He exem-
plifies it all: the change and the issue from it. After his three
years of first discipleship, in the strength of his young adulthood, came, how abruptly!, his mid-life crisis. And it was
indeed a crisis. It was indeed a case of, 'He has broken my
strength in mid-course'. 'And he broke down and wept' (Mk
14:72). Does his denial nullify all that went before? Certainly
not. But it did expose the ambiguity. There was love, great
love, but more *amor concupiscentiae* than genuine *amor
benevolentiae*, more possessive love than oblative love. Jesus
was going to benefit Peter. 'Look, we have left everything and
followed you. What then will we have?' (Mt 19:27). It wasn't
the girl or the servants or the cold that unmanned him on the
night. It was, in a real sense, Jesus himself. Peter had a notion
of 'the Christ', and here was 'the Christ' getting it wrong,
doing the opposite, yielding to 'the power of darkness' (Lk
22:53). That's what broke Peter. 'You are the Christ' (Mk
8:29), he had said. And now he no longer was. It was a case
of 'You have taken away my God!' What defence had he left
against the natural fear of death, the natural desire to save his

skin? 'I do not know this man you are talking about' (Mk 14:71). 'He has broken my strength in mid-course.' 'The Lord turned and looked at Peter ... And he went out and wept bitterly' (Lk 22:61, 62).

> A lost thing could I never find,
> Nor a broken thing mend:
> And I fear I shall be all alone
> When I get towards the end.
> Who will there be to comfort me
> Or who will be my friend?[4]

Who can find the lost and mend the broken? One only! One broken in mid-course himself, now raised and constituted Son of God in power by the Father. 'When they had finished breakfast, Jesus said to Simon Peter, "Simon, son of John, do you love me more than these?"' (Jn 21:15). Surely this lakeside scene alone proves the divinity of the Gospel. If you are having a mid-life crisis, read John 21:1–23. Our Lord arranges everything: the catch, the breakfast, Peter, the beloved disciple. This is Peter being found, mended, comforted. This is Peter being given the rest of his life. What is happening?

First, Jesus. 'It is the Lord! ... Lord, you know everything' (vv. 7, 17). Second, love. 'Simon, son of John, do you love me?' (v. 15). Third, death. 'He said this to indicate the kind of death by which he would glorify God' (v. 19). Fourth, mission, work. 'Feed my lambs' (v. 15). Fifth, 'What is that to you? Follow me!' (v. 22). The one thing necessary.

First, Jesus – himself broken in mid-course and now made the beginning of the new creation. Before, there was ambiguity in Peter's soul. Who was driver? Who was passenger? Now it is clear. 'The Lord is my shepherd'. Before, Peter was the subject of the sentence, 'I will lay down my life for you.' Now, 'Lord you know everything, you know that I love you' (v. 17). He's happy as a subordinate clause. Before, Peter knew who Peter was. 'I will never deny you.' Now, 'Lord, you know everything.' You know me better than I know myself. From now on, faith is something other and more, and

Jesus is raised to a new sovereignty in the soul.

Second, love. Three times Peter is asked. The answer is his, but it's also Jesus who gives it. The love of God is poured into a heart by the Holy Spirit who is given, and the heart can only be poured out as a libation. The rest of life – the second journey – is simply opportunity for love. *Amor concupiscentiae* is at last overtaken by *amor benevolentiae*; need-love by gift-love. '[A]t this time ... the gift of self is made to God more genuinely and with greater generosity'.[5] The wound remains, the memory, but at the same time as remaining, it's healed, like Jesus' wounds. And another strange paradox is that though Jesus is greater in the eyes of the soul, imperially so, he is also closer. The love is more awesome, but it's also more tender. *Phileis me?* 'Do you love me?' The sovereignty of Jesus is the sovereignty of love.

Third, death. Another gift. It's possible now for Jesus to give Peter his death, and it's possible for Peter now to accept the very thing he had run away from.

> Truly, truly, I say to you, when you were young, you girded yourself and walked where you would; but, when you are old, you will stretch out your hands, and another will gird you and carry you where you do not wish to go (v. 18).

Thanks to Jesus, thanks to Jesus' death, which his will copy, thanks to his resurrection, Peter, when the hour comes, can let himself be handed over in turn into the hands of men, knowing that beneath them is the hand of God raising to life. The mention of 'glorifying' is crucial. It is a change of perspective. It means the horizon is now eternal life, more and more so from now on. 'On earth, the broken arch; in heaven, the perfect round' (R. Browning). The sovereignty of Jesus is the sovereignty of hope.

Fourth, the charge, the mission. 'Feed my lambs ... Tend my sheep ... Feed my sheep' (vv. 15, 16, 18). Doesn't the pastoral, all but maternal, imagery suggest, enable a quite new tenderness towards others? Rough Peter gentled ... Certainly, a mission is confirmed. And the job will be done now, not for what it gives the one who does it (though it will give, as well as take, more and more), but for love of the one who gives it. The work of the Lord is done for the Lord of the work. The love of Christ is proved in the love of the Church. The gift of self 'extends to others with greater serenity and wisdom, as well as with greater simplicity and richness of grace. This is the gift and experience of spiritual fatherhood and mother-hood.'[6]

Fifth, there is significance even in that last, strange exchange between Peter and his Lord about the beloved disciple (who was, after all, one of the sheep). 'When Peter saw him, he said to Jesus, "Lord, what about him?"' (v. 21). No! 'If it is my will that he remain until I come, what is that to you? Follow me!' (v. 22). There is no longer need to be omniscient, to be in control. Jesus disposes of everything. The one thing necessary is to follow. The one thing necessary is obedience. It is as simple as that.

I'm not suggesting that if you're fifty-five, this is how you'll be! I'm simply saying that what Jesus did to Peter after breakfast by the lake, he is willing to do to each of us. Our 'change' can be filled by his Passover.

'A lost thing could I never find,/Nor a broken thing mend.' Only Christ can 'take the curve' in us. Only he can ride out the storm. Only he can put Humpty-Dumpty together again. If there is a new straight beyond the curve, and peace beyond the turbulence, and wholeness after breaking, it's from him and in him. It *is* him, sovereign in us. It is the Holy Spirit known now to be, mysteriously, at the centre of the wound, in the crack. If someone the same but different, more accepting, more free, emerges from the crucible, it's only because Jesus, risen and ascended, lives and reigns, more accepted, more free in our hearts. May we be Peters to him!

Notes

1. Barbara Reynolds, *Dorothy L. Sayers: Her Life and Soul* (Hodder & Stoughton, London, 1993), p. 347.
2. William Johnston, *Being in Love* (Collins, London, 1988), chs 11 & 12 (1988); 'Isaac Regained', ch. 15 from *The Wound of Love: A Carthusian Miscellany* (Gracewing, Leominster, 1994); a column of Fr. Ronald Rolheiser's (2003); *Vita Consecrata*, n. 70 (1994).

3. Jean Vanier, *Community and Growth* (Paulist, New York, 1989), p. 140.
4. Hilaire Belloc, 'The South Country', from *Collected Poems* (Pimlico, London, 1991), p. 36.
5. John Paul II, *Vita Consecrata*, 70 (CTS, London, 1996).
6. Ibid.

11

'There We Must Stand'

Reflections on the Eucharistic Action

*[W]e go to the table. This is the perfection of the life in Christ;
for those who attain it there is nothing lacking for the blessed-
ness which they seek. It is no longer death and the tomb and
a participation in the better life which we receive, but the risen
One Himself . . .*

*As He washes them in baptism He cleanses them from the
dirt of wickedness and imposes His own form upon them; when
He anoints them [in the sacrament of Confirmation] He acti-
vates the energies of the Spirit . . . But when He has led the
initiate to the table and has given him His Body to eat He
entirely changes him, and transforms him into His own state.
The clay is no longer clay when it has received the royal likeness but is already the Body of the King. It is impossible to
conceive of anything more blessed than this.*

*It is therefore the final Mystery as well, since it is not possi-
ble to go beyond it or to add anything to it . . . After the
Eucharist then, there is nowhere further to go. There we must
stand, and try to examine the means by which we may preserve
the treasure to the end.*

Thus wrote the fourteenth-century Greek lay theologian,
Nicholas Cabasilas in the opening pages of Book IV of *The
Life in Christ*.[1]

'Thing' and Action

The word 'Eucharist' – from the Greek for 'thanksgiving' – is used in two senses. It may refer to the consecrated bread and wine, therefore to the Body and Blood of Christ contained, offered and received in this sacrament. Or it may refer to the liturgy of the Mass as a whole, and more particularly to its second part, the Liturgy of the Eucharist.

In the first sense, 'Eucharist' denotes a 'thing', indeed the 'most holy Thing' (the *Sanctissimum*): the elements of bread and wine once they have been consecrated, the Body and Blood of the Lord. Not a 'mere thing', therefore, but a Person, Christ himself, sacramentally present under the appearances of the consecrated bread and wine, offering his own body and pouring out his own blood. 'For in the most blessed Eucharist is contained the whole spiritual good of the Church, namely Christ himself our Pasch and the living bread which gives life to men through his flesh – that flesh which is given life and gives life through the Holy Spirit.'[2]

In the second sense, 'Eucharist' denotes a ritual, and so an *action*. Indeed, it denotes the most sacred action conceivable, the flaming heart of the world, no less. '*Do* this in memory of me,' says the Lord. '*Do* this, as often as you drink it, in remembrance of me' (1 Cor 11:25). So the Anglican liturgist Gregory Dix could say, 'The apostolic and primitive church regarded the Eucharist as primarily an *action,* something "done".'[3] And again, 'The ancients ... habitually spoke of "*doing* the Eucharist", (*eucharistiam facere*), "*performing* the mysteries" (*mysteria telein*), "*making* the synaxis" (*synaxin agein, collectam facere*) and "*doing* the oblation" (*oblationem facere, prosphoran poiein*).'[4] The very word 'sacrifice', so often used in the context, implies a doing: a 'making-sacred'.

It is to the Eucharist in this sense that the following reflections are given.

The Agents

Clearly, bishops and priests – the qualified celebrants – *do* the Eucharist in a special sense. Without them there can be no valid celebration of the Eucharist. Yet the Eucharist is, no less visibly, something in which all present take part, all do. '*All* have their own active parts to play in the celebration, each in his own way: readers, those who bring up the offerings, those who give communion, and the whole people whose "Amen" manifests their participation' (*Catechism* 1348). It has been the great achievement of the post-conciliar liturgical reform to make this more possible. But further, to the eyes of faith, there are invisible participants as well. The saints are commemorated, and not as past or absent, the dead still in process of purification, are prayed for, while the Preface of the Roman Eucharistic Prayers as it leads into the *Sanctus* conjures up 'concelebrating' angels and archangels. 'When, then, we celebrate the eucharistic sacrifice we are most closely united to the worship of the heavenly Church' (*Lumen Gentium* 50). Above all, the Eucharist is an action of Christ, the High Priest of the New Covenant, 'the same now offering himself through the ministry of priests who then offered himself on the cross', as one Church Council put it. So, 'the celebration of Mass [is] the action of Christ and the People of God hierarchically ordered.' And, 'in it is found the high point both of the action by which God sanctifies the world in Christ and of the worship that the human race offers to the Father, adoring him through Christ, the Son of God, in the Holy Spirit.'[5] The Eucharist is an action of Christ and the whole Church, however humble its here and now realization. And, by faith and baptism, we are qualified to take part in it, to join in the action.

The Liturgy of the Word

This action is in two parts. We speak of the Liturgy of the Word and the Liturgy of the Eucharist. As the Jewish convert,

Jean-Marie Cardinal Lustiger, once pointed out, the Liturgy of the Word represents a Christianization of the Synagogue service of readings, and the Liturgy of the Eucharist a Christian fulfilment of the Jewish ritual meal, specifically the Passover.

The essential element of the Liturgy of the Word is, of course, the biblical readings themselves. These follow a clear sequence: First Reading – Psalm – (Second Reading) – Acclamation before the Gospel – the Gospel reading itself. The deeper movement here is from Prophets (that is, the Old Testament) to Apostles (that is, the New Testament) and finally to Christ himself (the Gospel), a recapitulation of the history of the Judaeo-Christian revelation. Appropriate silence, the homily, the profession of faith and bidding prayers may further enhance, unfold, answer and turn to prayer what is heard in the readings. The essential action here for us as participants is that of listening, an art in itself, and here inwardly sensitized by the Holy Spirit.

The climax of the Liturgy of the Word is, needless to say, the reading of the Gospel, that is, of a portion from one of the four canonical Gospels: Matthew, Mark, Luke and John. This is signified by its restriction to an ordained minister, often by a special book containing the Gospel readings (an Evangeliary), by the prayers the reader is to say before and after, and by the use of incense and lights. 'This reading of the liturgic Gospel is something more than a mere instruction of the faithful. It is a vital moment in the sacred action of the Church. In it Christ the Energetic Word speaks and acts.' It is a moment when we 'are confronted by the awful realism of Christ. Here the Supernatural meets us, disclosed in the degree in which we can bear it, by human acts and human words'. We are offered a 'mysterious contact with the mind and heart of the Incarnate ... who comes forth again and again in His changeless Gospel, as in His earthly ministry, to teach men the secrets of Reality, to enlighten, heal and redeem.'[6]

The relationship between the Liturgy of the Word and the Liturgy of the Eucharist to which it leads has been well expressed thus:

The Church is nourished spiritually at the table of God's Word and at the table of the Eucharist: from the one it grows in *wisdom* and from the other in *holiness*. In the Word of God, the divine covenant is *announced*; in the Eucharist the new and everlasting covenant is *renewed*. The spoken Word of God *brings to mind* the history of salvation; the Eucharist *embodies* it in the sacramental signs of the liturgy. It can never be forgotten, therefore, that the divine Word read and proclaimed by the Church in the liturgy has as its one goal the sacrifice of the New Covenant and the banquet of grace. The celebration of Mass in which the Word is *heard* and the Eucharist is *offered and received* forms but one single act of divine worship.[7]

God's word is proclaimed and heard. Christ's Body and Blood are made present, offered and received. The former action prepares for the latter; the latter completes the former.

There is an ancient tradition of interpretation of the Mass which sees its *pattern* as an echo of the pattern of Christ's life. This should not be forced beyond a certain point, but it need not be simply scorned. Surely the movement of the Mass from teaching to sacrifice reflects the movement of Christ's public life, and makes of it for us always something of a 'going up', in his wake, to Jerusalem, the place of death and resurrection.

The Altar

The Liturgy of the Word completed, the Liturgy of the Eucharist begins. The Eucharist, being the Church's imitation of the Last Supper, necessarily calls for a table. When the Eucharist is celebrated in a church, that table becomes an altar. And it is especially at this moment of the Mass, when the altar is prepared and the gifts are brought, that the altar shines out.

Altars are as old as man, at least, it is said, since he ceased to be a hunter-gatherer: some humble and domestic, others public and magnificent, like the Altar to Zeus at Pergamon or the Ara Pacis of Caesar Augustus. How often children build secret altars! The Christian altar keeps, first of all, the memory of these deep and ancient things, of these sacred centres, 'high places', places of sacrifice, where the divine touches man and man the divine. Then too the Christian altar recalls, gathers up in itself the many altars of biblical tradition:

- the altar Noah built emerging from the Ark after the Flood (Gen 8:20);
- the altars Abraham set up in silence in the Promised Land whenever the Lord appeared to him (Gen 12:7; 13:18), and above all the terrible one on which he binds Isaac and receives him back (Gen 22:9–14);
- the stone Jacob anointed on waking from his nocturnal theophany: 'How awesome is this place! This is none other than the house of God, and this is the gate of heaven' (Gen 28:17);
- the altar, and twelve pillars, Moses erects at the foot of Mt Sinai, for the ratifying of the covenant of the Exodus (Ex 24:3ff.);
- the altars of burnt offering and incense in the Jerusalem Temple, places of Israel's daily sacrifice.

'As the variety of foreshadowing figures ceases', though, it is 'in Christ that the mystery of the altar is brought to fulfilment', as the Latin rite's Prayer of Dedication of an Altar beautifully expresses it. Above all, a Christian altar points to Christ: to his *person*, to him as the Living Altar, as the 'living stone' (1 Pet 2:4) in which we are to be built as 'a spiritual house' (1 Pet 2:5), as the 'cornerstone in whom the whole structure is joined together and grows into a holy temple' (Eph 2:20–1), as 'the spiritual Rock' from which we drink (1 Cor 10:4). So too it recalls the central *actions* of his life: it symbolizes, *is one with* the table of the Last Supper, the 'holy Table' as it is known in the East; it evokes the altar (the tree) of the Cross; it also stands in continuity with the Empty Tomb, the place from which eternal life entered the world.

Here [then, in a Christian altar] is the true high place, where Christ's sacrifice is continually offered in sacramental form, perfect praise is given You and our redemption is disclosed. Here the Lord's Table is prepared, at which Your children, nourished by the Body of Christ, are gathered into the one, holy Church.

> Here the faithful drink Your Spirit from the rivers flowing from
> Christ, the spiritual Rock, and become through him, a holy offer-
> ing, a living altar (Preface for the Rite of Dedication of an Altar).

Given this wealth of significance, it is no wonder that Christian altars have long been the object of liturgies of dedication
or consecration – with solemn prayers and washings, anoint-
ings, incensations, 'vestings', lights. No wonder they receive
reverence, especially the holy kiss, during the many liturgies
of which they are the centre. Monastic tradition has always
preserved a sense of this, and has recognized the altar as a
special focus of personal prayer, as well as of liturgical. In all
these rites and gestures, the altar is being acknowledged as if
it were a person, that is the person of Christ.

The Liturgy of the Eucharist

The Liturgy of the Eucharist proper – the second part of the
action – moves through three phases: the Preparation of the
Gifts, the Eucharistic Prayer, and the Rite of Communion.
The reflections that follow will also move through three parallel phases, beginning with what is most immediate and visible,
then touching on the core and centre of 'what is happening',
and moving thence to where all this ultimately leads, its final
goal or effect.

'Do this in memory of me.'

The Liturgy of the Eucharist is first of all an obedience to
these words of Jesus at the Last Supper. It is doing what he
did. It is an *imitation of Christ*. The Lord's Supper of Christian tradition (1 Cor 11:20) re-enacts Christ's Last Supper.
'We do exactly as the Lord did,' said St Cyprian of Carthage.
    At the Last Supper, held within the framework of the
Jewish Passover, Jesus took bread, blessed God, broke it,
gave it to his disciples and said, 'Take, eat; this is my body',
and then, later in the meal, took a cup of wine, gave thanks,
gave it to his disciples, and said, 'Drink of it, all of you; for

this is my blood ... ' (cf. Mt 26:26–9; Mk 14:22–5; Lk 22:19–21; 1 Cor 11:23–6).

> Accordingly, the Church has arranged the entire celebration of the Liturgy of the Eucharist in parts corresponding to precisely these words and actions of Christ:
>
> 1. At the Preparation of the Gifts, the bread and wine with water are brought to the altar, the same elements that Christ took into his hands.
> 2. In the Eucharistic Prayer, thanks are given to God for the whole work of salvation, and the offerings become the Body and Blood of Christ.
> 3. Through the fraction and through Communion, the faithful, though they are many, receive from the one bread the Lord's Body and from the one chalice the Lord's Blood in the same way the Apostles received them from Christ's own hands.[8]

Historically, the basic pattern of the Liturgy of the Eucharist, received from the Apostles, has been developed in the seven major liturgical traditions of the Church: Alexandrine, West Syrian, East Syrian, Armenian, Byzantine, Milanese and Roman. These vary in secondary matters but concur on the essentials.

This whole action, if it is to be a true doing of what Christ did, must be celebrated by a bishop (a successor of the apostles) or by a priest under a bishop's authority. Such a one, by the grace of the Holy Spirit received through the laying-on of hands, holds the place in the Lord's Supper which Christ held at the Last and acts in the person of Christ. He is the visible representative of the invisible Presider, Celebrant, Priest, his icon. He stands, as it were, at the head of the table, like the father of a family. His task is to do what Jesus did.

At this first level, the Eucharist appears very clearly as a *sacred meal*. Many deep human and biblical things could be said at this point: about bread and wine, and about eating and eating together, about the significance of meals in the Old Testament, about the Passover. The Mass presupposes and incorporates all of this, just as Jesus did by making a meal the farewell action of his life, and an ultimate expression of his care for his disciples. At this first, largely outward level, which the theologians call the *sacramentum tantum*, the Liturgy of the Eucharist is the Church's repetition of Christ's action in the Upper Room. It is an obedience to his words, 'Do this in memory of me.'

But what, beyond appearances, is 'this'?

> *'This is my Body which is given for you ...*
> *this is my Blood ... which is poured out.'*

With these words, the words of consecration spoken at the heart of the Eucharistic Prayer, we approach the sacred centre of the celebration, visible only to the eyes of faith, that which the theologians call the *res et sacramentum* (the reality in the sign).

At the Last Supper, Christ *anticipated* his Passover, the offering he would make of himself to the Father for us on the Cross, revealed as salvific in his resurrection.

In the Eucharist, the Church *commemorates* Christ's Passover and sacrifice. This commemoration has always been understood as more than subjective (mental), it is also objective (real, 'out there').

At the heart of the Eucharistic Prayer, the celebrant, empowered by the gift of the Holy Spirit received at ordination, after asking the same Spirit of God the Father in the prayer called the *epiclesis*, recounts the story of the Last Supper and, taking successively the bread and the chalice into his hands, speaks the words Christ himself spoke. Through this ministry of the priest, the bread and wine, while retaining their outward characteristics, are transformed (trans-substantiated) by the words of Christ and the action of the Holy Spirit into Christ's Body and Blood, and the living Christ makes present in sacramental signs the sacrifice he once offered to the Father on the Cross. At the heart of the Eucharistic action, therefore, it is the action of Christ himself which predominates.

Christ thus gives his whole self and his sacrifice to the Church, making it hers (ours) as well.

The faithful present, led by the celebrant, now *offer* the consecrated bread and wine, now the Body and Blood of

Christ, in prayer to God the Father. They do this above all in *thanksgiving* for the whole divine work of creation and redemption and in *intercession* for the Church and the whole world, for the living and the dead. They will finally *receive* the holy gifts in communion.

All of this makes the Eucharist at once the sacramental representation of the sacrifice of Christ, and the sacrifice of the Church herself. 'Christ's sacrifice present on the altar makes it possible for all generations of Christians to be united with his offering' (*Catechism* 1368).

Imaginatively, we may see any Eucharistic celebration as a raising up, in the here and now of countless times and places, of the Tree of the Cross (the Tree of Life), its fruit made ours in Holy Communion. Thus we 'proclaim the Lord's death until he comes' (1 Cor 11:26), and are united with the Passover of Christ.

But then a further question arises, where is all this leading?

> *'. . . We who are many are one body,*
> *for we all partake of the one bread.'*

What is the ultimate purpose, goal, effect of each and every Eucharist, what the theologians call the *res tantum* (the reality alone)?

Here we must recall the ultimate intentions of God for humanity, our intended, corporate destiny, as glimpsed for instance by John: 'He showed me the holy city Jerusalem coming down out of heaven from God, having the glory of God' (Rev 21:10–11). In every celebration of the Eucharist, however humble or small, this final situation – 'having the glory of God' – is both symbolized and genuinely anticipated. In every Eucharist, this 'End' is at once present as a reality (we share in the heavenly liturgy) and at work drawing us, in the measure of our openness, closer to our full appropriation of that reality.

The goal and completion of the Eucharistic action is not on the altar, but in *us*. Its final effect is the *Church*, in the most ample sense of that word. This shines out most clearly in the act of Eucharistic communion.

This can be variously expressed. One can describe the teleology of the Eucharist in terms of the sealing of the Covenant and our entry into it as the People of God, or in terms of the coming of the kingdom and the gathering together of 'the children of God who are scattered abroad' (Jn 11:52), or in terms of the Temple where God dwells with us and we with him, or in terms of the marriage of the Lamb and the banquet that celebrates it. Or again, in terms of both looking forward to the heavenly banquet in the world to come and already taking part in it. And precisely because of all this, the Eucharist has a transforming potential even for human society here and now.

Perhaps, though, the simplest and most effective way of capturing the purpose of it all is by evoking the full meaning of the term, the Body of Christ. 'The bread which we break, is it not a participation in the body of Christ? Because there is one bread, we who are many are one body, for we all partake of the one bread' (1 Cor 10:16–17). In the Eucharist Christ gives himself in his (sacramental) body and in that way makes us his ('mystical') body. As St Augustine and St Leo and several post-communion prayers pithily express it: 'we become what we receive.' We receive the Body of Christ and so become the Body of Christ. 'If therefore you are the Body of Christ and his members,' said St Augustine, 'it is your mystery placed on the Lord's Table; it is your Mystery that you receive.' 'He who suffered for us has entrusted to us in this sacrament his Body and Blood, which indeed he has even made for us. For we have been made his Body, and, by his mercy, we are that which we receive.'[9] 'Through one body, which is his own,' wrote St Cyril of Alexandria, 'he blesses by a mysterious communion those who believe in him, and he makes them concorporal with himself and with one another.'[10]

The *res tantum* of the Eucharist, says St Thomas on more than one occasion, is 'the unity of the mystical body'. It is the same thought. And this one Body, 'the fullness of him who fills all in all' (Eph 1:22), is the goal to which, through the Eucharist above all, the whole creation moves and the whole working of God is taking us.

For a lyrical evocation of this, it is hard to beat a short story, 'The Treading of Grapes', by the Orcadian writer

George Mackay Brown. Its final pages record a homily on the wedding feast at Cana imagined as having been preached in a parish church in Orkney in the late Middle Ages by a Father Halcrow.[11]

Dear children, this I have spoken of is a most famous marriage. We are poor people, fishermen and crofters, and we think it is not likely in these the days of our vanity that we will be bidden to such a feast. We are poor people, Olaf the fisherman and Jock the crofter and Merran the hen-wife, we are pleased enough with oatcakes and ale at our weddings, we were born to hunger and meikle hardship, and there will be a single candle burning beside us the night they come to straik us and to shroud us.

No, but this is not true. Let me tell you a secret. Christ the King, he hath uplifted our fallen nature as miraculously as he clothed water in the red merry robes of wine. Very rich and powerful you are, princes, potentates, heirs and viceroys of a Kingdom. So opulent and puissant are you, dear ones, for that each one of you has in his keeping an immortal soul, a rich jewel indeed, more precious than all the world beside. So then, princes (for I will call you Olaf the fisherman and Jock the crofter no longer but I will call you by the name the Creator will call you in the last day) princes, I say, I have good news for you, you are bidden every one to a wedding. Get ready your gifts, get ready your shoes to the journey. *What wedding?* you ask, *we know of no wedding.* I answer, *The marriage of Christ with His Church. And where will this marriage be?* you ask. *Everywhere*, I answer, *but in particular, lords and princes, in this small kirk beside the sea where you sit. And when is it to be, this wedding?* you ask me. *Always*, I answer, *but in particular within this hour, now, at the very moment when I bow over this bread of your offering, the food, princes and lords, that you have won with such hard toil from the furrows, at once when I utter upon it five words* HIC EST ENIM CORPUS MEUM. Then is Christ the King come once again to his people, as truly as he was present at the marriage in Cana, and the Church his bride abides his coming, and this altar with the few hosts on it and the cup is a rich repast indeed, a mingling of the treasures of earth and heaven, and the joy of them in Cana is nothing to the continual merriment of the children of God. *Sanctus sanctus sanctus,* they cry forever and ever, *Benedictus qui venit in nomine Domini.*

Dance ye then, princes and ladies, in your homespun, there is no end to this marriage, it goes on at every altar of the world, world without end. This Bread that I will raise above your kneeling, It is entire Christ – Annunciation, Nativity, Transfiguration, Passion, Death, Resurrection, Ascension, Majesty, gathered up into one perfect offering, the Divine Love itself, whereof you are witnesses.

And not only you, princes, all creation rejoices in the marriage of Christ and His Church, animals, fish, plants, yea, the water, the wind, the earth, the fire, stars, the smallest grains of dust that blow about your cornfields and your Kirkyards.

In Nomine Patris et Filii et Spiritus Sancti. Amen.

Notes

1. Nicolas Cabasilas, *The Life in Christ* (St Vladimir's Seminary Press, New York, 1974), pp. 113–114.
2. Second Vatican Council, *Presbyterorum Ordinis* 5.
3. Gregory Dix, *The Shape of the Liturgy* (A. & C. Black Ltd, London, 1945), p. 15.
4. Ibid., p. 12.
5. *General Instruction of the Roman Missal*, rev. 2002 (CTS, London, 2005), 16.
6. Evelyn Underhill, *The Mystery of Sacrifice* (Longmans, London, 1944), pp. 9–10.
7. *General Introduction to the Lectionary*, 2nd edition, n.10, (my italics).
8. *General Instruction of the Roman Missal*, 72.
9. St Augustine, Sermons 272, 229.
10. St Cyril of Alexandria, *On John* 11, 11.
11. George Mackay Brown, 'A Treading of Grapes' (reproduced by kind permission of the executors of George Mackay Brown's estate).

12

Brotherhood

In chapter 63, St Benedict urges the older monks to call the younger ones, easily overlooked in that world, by the title of 'brother' (*Rule* 63.12). Similar echoes can be caught, Vogüé notes, in other sixth-century monastic writings: a concern to make of this ancient Christian word a title of courtesy preceding proper names.

'One day I realized these blokes were my brothers,' one of the brethren once said, recording a personal breakthrough. Yes, not obstacles, not enemies, but brothers. In the Rule the word 'brother' is used more than 'monk'.

So, what do we understand by the words 'brother', 'brotherly', 'brotherhood'? What does it mean to 'be a brother', a brother to others, to say to others: 'I am Joseph your brother' (Gen 45:4)?

Let me try some reflections on the theme of brotherhood.

Alternatives

For the Christian, brotherhood suggests the Church. But it is not alone on stage. How does it relate to the other brotherhoods that are about? Joseph Ratzinger published a very thoughtful little book on all this in the 1960s, *Christian Brotherhood*. The Enlightenment made much of the 'brotherhood of man'. Ironically, one of the consequences, from the French Revolution on, was a succession of pseudo-universal brotherhoods with truly astounding quantities of blood on their hands, illustrating the truth of Jonathan Sacks' understated remark: 'it is precisely when [fraternity] is conceived as a political value that it begins to lose all human resonance.'[1] At their worst such 'big brotherhoods' become a dehumanizing, diabolical parody of true unity. Even when less than worse they seem incapable, for all their apparent tolerance, of tolerating the particular. Then, at the other extreme, there are the micro-brotherhoods of free-masonries and mafias, terrorist cells and cults, ethnic groups, even nations – representing the brotherhood of the elect; hostile, exclusive particularisms, closed to the universal.

In both extremes, the brotherhood that, even after Cain and Abel, is innate to humanity, innate as a reality that must be lived out, a gift and a task, expressed in recognition of a universal moral law, in traditions of hospitality, instincts of compassion, principles of justice, and a crying imperative in a globalizing world, is being obscured. Jews and Christians – I cannot speak for Muslims – looking at the realm of nature through the eyes of grace have become, I feel, such a threatened brotherhood's best champions. This is the brotherhood which many nineteenth-century Russian Christians spoke up for, shocked with Fyodorov that 'there are people who are not kindred but strangers, and that even some kindred are strangers one to another'; or of which, two world wars later, *Gaudium et Spes* gently but starkly said: 'Before the contemporary world stands a choice of ways: to brotherhood or hatred.'

'The "brotherhood of man", as an abstraction, is predicated on the belief that if we love no one in particular we will love everyone in general. The opposite is at least as likely to be the case,' says Rabbi Sacks.[2] Is there a brotherhood universal in a way other than the bland or vicious and particular in a way other than the exclusive?

Let me simply point to some of the bases of a Christian understanding and the Christian way.

The New Testament

To recall some passages of the New Testament, first of all:

> Who is my mother and who are my brethren? And stretching out his hand toward his disciples, he said, Here are my mother and my brethren. For whoever does the will of my Father in heaven is my brother and sister and mother (Mt 12:48–50).

> But you are not to be called rabbi, for you have one teacher, and you are all brethren (Mt 23:8).

> And the King will answer them, Truly I say to you, as you did it to one of the least of these my brethren, you did it to me (Mt 25:40).

> Truly, I say to you, there is no one who has left house or brothers or sisters or mother or father or children or lands for my sake and for the gospel, who will not receive a hundredfold now in this time, houses and brothers and sisters ... (Mk 10:29–30).

> Go to my brethren and say to them, I am ascending to my Father and your Father, to my God and your God (Jn 20:17).

> Those whom he foreknew he also predestined to be conformed to the image of his Son, in order that he might be the first-born among many brethren (Rom 8:29).

> For he who sanctifies [that is, Christ] and those who are sanctified all have one origin. That is why he is not ashamed to call them brethren (Heb 2:11).

> We know that we have passed out of death into life, because we love the brethren ... Anyone who hates his brother is a murderer ... By this we know love, that he laid down his life for us; and we ought to lay down our lives for the brethren (1 Jn 3:14, 15, 16).

The Christians of the apostolic age, clearly, knew they were brothers one to another. They were such because sons of the

Father, now, by faith and baptism. They addressed each other accordingly: 'Brother Saul,' says Ananias boldly (Acts 9:17). They accepted the duties of mutual concern and forbearance, the *philadelphia* this new dignity entailed. They had the bitter experience of the 'false brother' and the sweet experience of 'brotherly love'. They called the Church the 'brotherhood' (1 Pet 2:17; 5:9), and it was by the use of the phrase 'the brethren' that the Jewish Christians graciously acknowledged the truth of the Gentiles' call to faith: 'The brethren, both the apostles and the elders, to the brethren who are of the Gentiles in Antioch and Syria and Cilicia' (Acts 15:23).

This brotherhood, however small at times, was not a 'holy huddle'. It was, in essence and scope, universal, a place where all the redeemed could find a home, especially the insignificant, the suffering, the unfortunate, the poor. And it was something new in human history, yet old too; it was the original brotherhood, lost since Cain and Abel, restored in Christ. At its centre stands the Son. In him we become sons of the one Father, and therefore brothers of and to one another.

'Then,' wrote St Justin Martyr, 'we conduct the newly-baptized into the assembly of those we call brothers.'[3]

In Christianity, as Joseph Ratzinger pointed out, we have a brotherhood that is neither un-really generalized and all-embracing nor crampingly, 'sectish-ly' particular. It is a brotherhood demarcated, concrete, specific enough to engage human sensibility, and, yes, claiming a divine election, but in essence and in destiny universal. If the called are few, relatively to the many, they are called, nonetheless, in relation to them, their 'other brothers', called to mission, to love, to suffering in their regard. They cannot possibly exclude. 'Hate no one,' says St. Benedict, and 'honour all men.'

Historically, it has been the monks, and then the friars, who have kept alive the idea of Christian brotherhood, in relation of course first of all to themselves. It has lain in their granaries, waiting for a time of wider sowing.

I'd like to suggest that in the last hundred years or so, this time has come, that there has been a movement of the Spirit prompting Christians to a fresh awareness of brotherhood, of the call to be brothers, to be Josephs not Cains. And this especially to those in whatever senses outside the Church's brotherhood. There's a thread here.

It was a significant moment when Leo XIII began referring to non-Catholic Christians as 'separated brethren'. In the Latin phrase, of course, the word 'brethren' comes first and has the emphasis upon it. It was an echo of St Augustine talking to the Donatists and his use of a particular version of Isaiah 66:5, 'Those who hate you . . . and do not want to be called your brothers, you though say to them: you are our brothers!'

But Charles de Foucauld, as so often, is a key figure – this 'little brother of Jesus'. By the Incarnation, he realized, the Son of God has become our brother, our elder brother, the first-born of many brethren. In 1902, at Beni-Abbes he wrote: 'I am in the house at Nazareth where, between Mary and Joseph, I am clasped like a little brother by his elder brother Jesus, present day and night in the Sacred Host.' Jesus being brother to us calls us to be brothers to everyone. And so in a letter of the same year: 'I want to accustom the inhabitants here, Christians, Muslims, Jews and idolaters, to regard me as their brother, the universal brother' – a famous phrase and an essential part of his spiritual message. 'Already they're calling this house "the fraternity", about which I'm delighted . . . and realizing that the poor have a brother here – not only the poor, though: everyone.' And four months before his death, in August 1916, he wrote: 'I do not think there is a Gospel phrase which has made a deeper impression on me and transformed my life more than this one: Insofar as you did this to the least of these brothers of mine, you did it to me.'

Poverty, as we know, was something dear to Foucauld. And poverty was for him imitation of Jesus and brotherhood with the poor. There we have a 'new' reading, it seems to me, of an evangelical counsel – in the light of brotherhood.

This thread – this being brother – can be picked up in two other modern saints. The prayer for the memorial of St Maximilian Kolbe mentions his 'zeal for souls and love of neighbour'. I was thinking when I heard it, Oh these wordy modern Collects! Then a penny dropped. 'Zeal for souls' summed up his whole apostolic life as a Conventual Franciscan in Poland and Japan, but 'love of neighbour' needed saying too. It refers to what he did at the very end, offering his life for Francis Gajowniczek. And the Alleluia we sing is: 'this is the true brotherhood which is stronger than the crimes of the world.' Yes, Kolbe showed himself a neighbour, was a brother to this condemned man. This was true brotherly love: to give his life in this man's place. And it struck me too that in the words passed at that moment, there was a new interpretation being given to the evangelical counsel of chastity, to celibacy. 'My wife and my children!' was Francis Gajowniczek's immediate reaction when he was chosen for the starvation bunker. Kolbe stood forward. 'Who are you?' asks the Commandant. 'A Catholic priest . . . I have no family.'

Then there's Edith Stein, St Teresa Benedicta of the Cross. Here the being brother (or sister) concerns the same people St Paul called 'my brethren according to the flesh'.

> I spoke with the Saviour [this is Easter 1933] to tell him that I realized it was his Cross that was now being laid upon the Jewish people, that the few who understood this had the responsibility of carrying it in the name of all, and that I myself was willing to do this, if he would only show me how.

Entering Carmel was a first step. She identified herself with Esther – how could she not? – brought near to the King for the sake of her Jewish brothers and sisters. Here the contemplative life is re-read as being brother/sister to the persecuted. Her blood sister, Rosa, joined her in the Carmel. There was a hope that they could transfer to the Swiss Carmel, Le Paquier. But there was only room for Edith. They couldn't take Rosa as well. This was unacceptable to Edith. But most striking is that last scene at the gate of the Echt Carmel, in the afternoon of Sunday 2 August 1942. A crowd, angry with the SS, had gathered, and Rosa who had, of course, been taken too, began to grow disoriented. Edith turned to her, took her hand, and said: 'Come, Rosa, give me your hand. We are going for our people.' And so the two sisters go to martyrdom hand in hand. And they die because they are Jews, because brethren according to the flesh with this persecuted people, and they die for the Jews, as brethren according to the Spirit. Being brother finally means 'suffering with'. Thanks to Edith, Pope John Paul II could call the Jews our 'elder brothers' – and open up another door.

The same thread runs again, surely, through the story of the seven monks of Tibhirine, Atlas, Algeria, beheaded by terrorists on 21 May 1996. These monks are, as their Abbot General has said, 'a word spoken by God'. And surely they died for brotherhood, in the very line of Foucauld, in the same Muslim world, victims of the same fanatical violence. There's a phrase in Fr Christian's Journal for 4 January 1995: 'the Son who is infinitely Brother'. And then in his Testament:

> If it should happen one day – and it could be today – that I become a victim of the terrorism which now seems ready to engulf all the foreigners living in Algeria, I would like my community, my Church and my family to remember that my life was GIVEN to God and to this country.

To God and to this country. It seems that this Cistercian community has given us a new reading of stability – in the light of brotherhood. They could have left. They chose to stay – to be with their Algerian and Muslim brothers. They wished to be the Church in Algeria for the Algerian people. 'There is a presence of God among men,' wrote Fr Christian in Lent 1996, 'which we ourselves must assume. It is in this perspective that we understand our vocation to be a fraternal presence of men and women who share the life of Muslims, of Algerians, in prayer, silence and friendship.' And so the famous ending to the Testament:

> And also you, my last-minute friend, who will not have known what you are doing [he was thinking of his future assassin]: Yes, I want this THANK YOU and this A-DIEU to be for you too, because in God's face I see yours. May we meet again as happy thieves in Paradise, if it please God, the Father of us both.[4]

There is a thread here, surely – in these nine men and one woman, all of them, be it noted, religious. A living out of the Incarnation to the point of the Cross for the sake of the 'brother' – or rather by *being* a brother. It is a way of being a Christian, of being Church, where the Christian and the Church find themselves a minority in an indifferent, even hostile world. It's a way for Christianity after Christendom. There's a Gospel simplicity about it. And it requires nothing less, to be real, than constant prayer: the eye on Christ, the hand for the brother.

So let us be brothers one to another, as best we can, shoulder to shoulder in the 'battle-line of brothers' (*Rule* 1.5). It is not only for ourselves.

Notes

1. Jonathan Sacks, *The Politics of Hope* (Vintage, London, 2000), p. 205.
2. Ibid.
3. St Justin Martyr, *Apology* I, 65, 1.
4. Bernardo Olivera, *How Far to Follow? The Martyrs of Atlas* (St Bede's Publications, Petersham, MA, 1997).

13

Mutual Reverence

I was greatly cheered recently by some guests saying how struck they were by the brethren's reverence for one another.

We live close together. As monasteries go, we have a lot of life in common. Mutual irritation is inevitable; 'the thorns of scandal . . .' A quantity of mutual exasperation is part of our daily bread. That's the way it is. And it's inevitable too that we have a fairly realistic appreciation of one another's weaknesses. Nor do many of us seem backward in articulating our insights. (As abbot, of course one can flatter oneself that it's all in the line of duty.) Is this because we're men? Is it because we live in Scotland, a traditionally free-speaking country? I don't know. I do think, though, that there is actually something healthy about this. At any rate, it needn't be automatically deplored. It can be quite compatible with mutual respect and appreciation. It's parallel to what happens in a healthy family life. Brothers and sisters may have no illusions about each other, nor parents about their children, and yet there's a bond stronger than death.

The story is told of an SAS man, subjected to verbal abuse by his captors during the first Gulf War, and realizing it would have no effect upon him whatsoever: he was so accustomed to receiving it from his comrades in the regiment!

Still, there are limits. The healthy can become unhealthy. The devil wants nothing so much as to alienate monk from monk, brother from brother, and if he can achieve this in our minds, he's already on the way to victory. There are three subordinate demons he can send on mission:

1. A certain blame-culture

The scenario is as follows: something 'wrong' is done (for example, someone should have been met at the airport, but wasn't; something should have been collected from the town, but wasn't; information should have been communicated, but wasn't). Immediately, the cry goes up, a mental cry at least, whistles are blown, the dogs are called out, the hunt is on – the quest for the victim, to be named and shamed. This is, as it were, the negative of chapter 46 of the Rule.

The ugly thing in all this, the sign of the cloven hoof, is the unspoken word: 'It wasn't me.' A victim has been found. Oh, the relief! But hasn't René Girard been proved right? *Tempus iracundiae non reservare*, says St Benedict: don't put an irritation away in your pocket for later use, don't fatten the dossier.

I exaggerate, but not wildly. I suppose monks are perfectionists, almost in a sense by profession, and therefore we react strongly to imperfection. It must be traced to its source. Or again, perhaps it's a love of justice, or the desire to know, 'the knowledge of things in their ultimate causes'. But the rider can so easily lose charge of the horse. The only answer to a culture of blame is a culture of forgiveness. That's clear as the day on the world stage, but might it not hold true on our stage too? Can't we just let some mistakes or mishaps go? Monks are, in my experience, very forgiving animals. Perhaps we just need to try to be so over the little things as well as the big.

2. The habit of judgement

On the ninth step of humility, we meet the famous proposal not to speak until a question arises. Taking that literally would lead to chaos. But it can be read and lived as an appeal not to pass judgement when judgement isn't needed.

How many – not necessarily rash or false, but simply uncalled-for – judgements we make! The monk of the twelfth step is absorbed by the thought of God's judgement on himself; most of us expend much energy on our judgements of others, or simply on matters which do not concern us.

Better to leave these things to the Lord and to those whose responsibility they actually are. I'm not advocating self-induced senility nor the life of an ostrich, just custody of the mental eyes. 'Whenever his thoughts urged him to pass judgement on something which he saw, he would say to himself, "Agathon, it is not your business to do that." Thus his spirit was always recollected.'[1]

Sins of the flesh impact upon us when we commit them; their factuality is hard to deny (though their guilt may not be). But it's possible to denigrate others and minutes later to have forgotten doing so. We sail blithely on. This is scary. 'You did these things, and I was silent.'

Mind separated from love, intelligence unwarmed by charity, bring us close to the diabolical. Sometimes one meets brilliant intelligence, but restless, unconnected, without reverence, the head no longer anchored in the heart. On the other hand, there can be the symbiosis of truth and love, insight and affection, clarity and kindness. Someone like Bl. Columba Marmion seemed to have that. Neither sentimental nor merely intellectual. Truth and love have embraced. That is the human ideal.

3. The attribution of motive

We see someone doing something and up goes the mental bubble: 'What's he up to? Ah, yes, of course ... There he goes again ... Typical.' And we assign a motive. Most rash judging is rash because of that. We all have our 'takes' on one another, and every fresh detail is pressed into its service. Generally the motive assigned is not too flattering. The sobering fact is we can be wrong. The demonic fact is we're playing God. 'Man judges by appearances but God sees the heart.' Best then to restrict ourselves to appearances – to take the facts as they present themselves – and leave the rest to God. If a further judgement is required, if we have the responsibility of discerning the spirits, then let us do so humbly and mindful of God.

We need to be especially careful about attributing motive

when we feel personally hurt by someone's action. If we're not, we can walk ourselves into a whole fantasy land.

One thing I've often observed: tell a young monk of some unfortunate episode in a monastery, and he will tend to pass judgement. 'Well, the wrong thing there was ... ' Tell an older monk, and he will probably say nothing. Blessed silence! Abba Xanthias said, 'A dog is better than I am, for he has love and he does not judge.'[2]

St Benedict is strong on reverence. Could we call it chastity of the mind? Blaming, judging, assigning motive are all, in a sense, failures to keep our mental hands off others, forgetting they belong to God, the one judge, and not primarily to me. 'Let them outdo one another in showing honour' is St Benedict's preferred way.

One more thought to conclude. I suppose what is happening here is that we are stumbling at the mystery of evil. We are trying to exorcize evil, but in fact becoming more possessed by it. We are seeing the splinter and missing our beam. But on the wood of the Cross, Christ converted evil from stumbling stone to stepping stone. And we must follow him in that.

It is part of the mystery of the hidden life – life lived under God's over-shadowing – that we experience in a particularly acute way our own sinfulness. It's the dark underside of the cloud of God's presence. In the hermit life, solitude will engender this experience. In the cenobitic life, community will. It little matters. In the parlour, or presiding at Mass, or giving a talk, we're the man of God. In our cells and with our brethren, we're closer to the man of sin, or the man under judgement. This can come at us in a variety of ways: consciousness of our own besetting sins, the sense that our brethren and superior don't think all that highly of us, even our difficulty in seeing holiness in our brethren. Years of prayer and fidelity may not yield any visible fruit. In fact, the fruit is hidden in God and hidden from us. It's the strange mystery of living in the *shadow* of God and His grace; living more conscious, for example, of what we lack than of what we have.

It is a very hard thing to bear. Everything in us wants to run away from it. Even the way we pursue holiness can be a running away from it. Faith, say the mystics – and faith is another name for what I'm talking about – is certainty in darkness. We have to come to the point, paradoxically, of being content, even glad, with the darkness. Then we don't stumble. Evil ceases to be a scandal. As St Bernard wrote:

> [It] is necessary for us in the meantime to lie hidden if we have a precious thing, for it is the treasure of the kingdom of heaven which a man found and hid away. That is why we hide bodily in cloisters and in forests. Do you wonder what we gain by this hiddenness? There is no one here, I believe, who, were he to do in the world a quarter of what he does here, would not be revered as a saint, reckoned as an angel, whereas now he is daily rebuked and chided as negligent. Do you think it no small advantage not to be taken for a saint before actually being one? ... it is necessary for all this to be hidden not only from other people's eyes, but from your own as well, and even more necessary ... In this lies great virtue and the best security: that while you live faithfully, forgetting what lies behind and straining forward to what lies ahead, you do not so much see what you have already obtained as wait for what you still lack. This hiddenness ... beneath the Lord's shoulders, is something very similar to the overshadowing which came upon Mary from the Holy Spirit to conceal an incomprehensible mystery.[3]

I also think of the Resurrection. It was made known in the day, it brought everlasting day, but it happened in the night – *O beata nox* – and nobody saw it.

Notes

1. *Sayings of the Desert Fathers* (Cistercian Publications, Kalamazoo, 1984), p. 23.
2. Ibid., p. 159.
3. St Bernard, *Sermons on Conversion*, Cistercian Fathers Series, 25 (Cistercian Publications, Kalamazoo, 1981), pp. 137–8.

14

Homily for Br Adrian's Golden Jubilee of Profession

3 May 2003

In the first reading, we heard St Paul solemnly proclaiming the Lord's resurrection. In the Gospel, we heard Jesus proclaiming his role as mediator: 'No one can come to the Father except through me.' I think that, keeping Dom Adrian's Golden Jubilee, we are hearing the same things. The Gospel is not meant to stay on the page; it's meant to pass into lives. And it has passed into Dom Adrian's life. 'No one can come to the Father except through me.' It is by the grace of the risen, indwelling Christ that our jubilarian has lived his fifty monastic years. God upholds his human creatures, and Christ upholds the monk, day after day, year after year.

We are grateful, most of all. Grateful to God, grateful to our unique and ineffable Dom Adrian. The garden which the monastery is, says Saint Aelred, is like the garden of paradise. In this garden, 'the different brethren are like fruitful trees', each bearing fruit according to its kind. One, he says, will stand out for humility, another for charity, another for patience, another for chastity, and another for working hard at manual labour (*Sermo* LIX, 25). There's our tree today! Dom Adrian shuffling out to the garden in all weathers, a good ten years over what the world calls 'retirement age'. Dom Adrian on a tractor, behind a rotivator, feeding the pigs or cats or chickens, digging up the early potatoes, carrying in the buckets of vegetables. In September 1951 he wrote to the Novice Master at Prinknash. 'I do ask you to let me come as soon as there is room ... I feel that in my case when I have already left the world once it is unwise to turn back on the plough.' A prophetic image!

> I knew [he might have said with John Masefield]
> That Christ was standing there with me,
> That Christ had taught me what to be.
> That I should plough, and as I ploughed
> My Saviour Christ would sing aloud,
> And as I drove the clods apart
> Christ would be ploughing in my heart,
> Through rest-harrow and bitter roots,
> Through all my bad life's rotten fruits.[1]

In opere manuum laboriosior ('painstaking in manual work'). 'Working with Dom Adrian is not an experience I'll ever forget,' says one former novice. He has even worked his way into Scottish literature, in a novel published in 1996:

> Then I rounded a bend and emerged from the trees and there it was – a full-scale medieval monastery, completely rebuilt and obviously in working order and fully functional! I gasped ... There's a spacious lawn on the near side, and to my right as I walked up, hidden behind a hedge, I discovered a little graveyard with plain wooden crosses ... Two men in working clothes crossed my path – monks, as I later discovered: one of them was very tall and gentle-looking, the other small and down to earth. I liked the look of them.[2]

Going on, allow me another quotation, this one from *The Lord of the Rings*. It's Sam the stout-hearted hobbit talking to Frodo.

> The brave things in the old tales and songs, Mr Frodo: adventures, as I used to call them. I used to think that they were things the wonderful folk of the stories went out and looked for, because they wanted them, because they were exciting and life was a bit dull, a kind of sport, as you might say. But that's not the way of it with the tales that really mattered, or the ones that stay in the mind. Folk seem to have been just landed in them, usually – their paths were laid that way, as you put it. But I expect they had lots of chances, like us, of turning back, only they didn't. And if they

had, we shouldn't know, because they'd been forgotten. We hear
about those as just went on . . .[3]

A good line for a golden jubilee! In the 1950s, before our jubilarian's solemn profession, one of his confreres confidently
maintained, 'He'll never stick it.' Well, 'we hear about those
as just went on.'

In 1948 a young man of twenty-two found himself in East
Africa, part of the post-World War II Labour government's
Ground Nuts Scheme in Tanganyika. He was not long
Catholic, and not long demobbed. And there he met a German
Benedictine mission, founded by the missionary Congregation
of St Ottilien. What attracted him, he said, was the sacrifice
these men were making – the generosity of it. And so he
offered himself – generously – to the Bishop, a Benedictine
monk. One might say: having helped defeat the Axis as a
Sapper, young Mr Walker now turned his attention to the
Devil. Ndanda, the place, is today a monastery of almost
seventy monks but was then just a mission. And so the Bishop
said: 'Go to a monastery of our Congregation in the USA.' He
did, and found himself landed in the adventure of his monastic life. Quite an odyssey it was to be. Seven novice masters
anyway. New Jersey, then Buckfast, then Prinknash where he
made his first profession fifty years ago. It was the fifteenth
anniversary of Wilfrid Upson's blessing as abbot, and just
over forty years after the conversion of the Caldey community. Then a time at Pluscarden; then to Farnborough. 'He has
never lost hope of one day being allowed to make his profession as a Benedictine monk,' said his last novice master in
1956, and this despite not making it in the States, not being
taken on at Buckfast, being regarded rather unfavourably up
here. 'This proves a great determination and a strong will.'
'Just keep knocking,' Fr Alban had said to him. And so, on
the feast of all holy monks, 13 November 1956, Fr Basil
received his solemn profession.

> O Christ who holds the open gate,
> O Christ who drives the furrow straight,
> O Christ, the plough, O Christ, the laughter

> Of holy birds flying after,
> Lo, all my heart's field red and torn,
> And Thou wilt bring the young green corn,
> The young green corn divinely springing,
> The young green corn forever singing.[4]

In 1964 he returned to Pluscarden and has been here ever since. Born in England, educated in Wales, a soldier in France, Belgium, Holland and Germany, a pioneer in Tanganyika, liable to tell you at recreation how much he enjoyed his stopover in Khartoum, a monk in the United States, England, and Scotland at last. '... their paths were laid that way, as you put it. But I expect they had lots of chances, like us, of turning back, only they didn't. And if they had, we shouldn't know, because they'd been forgotten. We hear about those as just went on ...' When I first entered, the young-looking Dom Adrian (I guessed he was thirty; in fact he was forty-eight) was a regular reader in choir and refectory. Novices and juniors would come. He'd be retired. They'd go. He'd come back. Up he'd get, and once again the voice would sound. One of those 'as just went on'. Dom Adrian ploughing on the tractor, playing at the organ, reading in choir, going down to the Burn on Sunday afternoon. These have been fixtures.

I'm grateful. God upholds his human creatures, and Christ upholds the monk. Dom Adrian has been a glimpse of the Gospel for me, and today he's a Eucharist. I've lived with him for nearly thirty years, I've never had an unkind word from him; and I have had many kindnesses – not to mention many vegetables. He has taught me a lot about the mystery of brotherhood. Accept a brother as he is, with his strengths and his weaknesses, and one is changed and enriched. I have a vow of conversion of life: the conversion of my life, not other people's. And I am converted when I let my brother in. Now, of course, in fifty years of monastic life, it isn't impossible that someone might, on the odd rare occasion, have been perhaps, possibly, infuriating (mildly, naturally). It is even remotely conceivable that in fifty years of monastic life, murder might have flickered through brethren's minds as the only possible solution. Once or twice at the most that is, over fifty years (and only at the bad moments of the day, like the first Nocturn of Vigils). But then, at such moments, back it comes, the mystery of brotherhood. The knife is sheathed as I remember, I love this man. This man who knows his weaknesses so well. This humble, truthful, hard-working man. He's a tree in the garden. He's part of the music Pluscarden makes. He's one of those as just goes on. He's himself, drawn by generosity in the beginning and generous ever since. He's unique. He's God's. He's Christ's. He's ours. He's Adrian our brother, in life and death. *Deo gratias*.

And what of the future? I hope he won't vanish into Eternity too soon. But it does strike me how many of the things he loves: music, liturgy, water, gardens, trees and animals, are part of the imagery of heaven. 'To commit one's hope to God', says St Benedict in any case. Let John Masefield end, the ploughman talking to Christ:

> And when the field is fresh and fair
> Thy blessed feet shall glitter there,
> And we will walk the weeded field,
> And tell the golden harvest's yield,
> The corn that makes the holy bread
> By which the soul of man is fed,
> The holy bread, the food unpriced,
> Thy everlasting mercy, Christ.[5]
> Amen.

Notes

1. John Masefield, *The Everlasting Mercy*, in *The Oxford Book of English Mystical Verse* (OUP, Oxford, 1921), pp. 552–5.
2. John Herdman, Ghost Writing (Polygon, Edinburgh, 1996), pp. 126–7.
3. J. R. R. Tolkien, *The Two Towers* (HarperCollins, London, 1991), p. 696.
4. Masefield.
5. Ibid.

Part III: Bearing Fruit

By contrast, the fruit of the Spirit is love, joy, peace, patience, kindness, goodness, faithfulness, gentleness, and self-control. There is no law against such things (Gal 5:22, NRSV).

15

Consolation

'When will you console me?' asks the Psalmist (Ps 118:82).
The period between the Ascension and the Second Coming is
the time of trial, and we, as Hebrews says, are in the midst of
our test. And so we cry out for consolation. We suffer; we
can't not. We are, even, what we have suffered. What we've
suffered and the way we have met it gives us whatever weight
we have. 'Suffering produces endurance, and endurance
produces character' (Rom 5:3–4). But in the suffering we need
consolation. We need it as individuals, as community, as
Church, as human beings in the Third Millennium. 'I yearn
for your saving help; I hope in your word. My eyes yearn to
see your promise. When will you console me?' (Ps 118:81–2).

'Blessed be the God and Father of our Lord Jesus Christ,
the Father of mercies and the God of all consolation,' says St
Paul, 'who consoles us in all our affliction, so that we may be
able to console those who are in any affliction with the consolation with which we ourselves are consoled by God' (2 Cor
1:3–4). There is the pattern: on the one hand affliction, on the
other consolation. To Boethius in his prison came the consolation of Philosophy, that is, Wisdom. As St Augustine
famously said,[1] the Church 'makes its pilgrim way between
the persecutions of the world and the consolations of God.'
And so, *mutatis mutandis*, does each of us. In every heart the
question rises up: 'When will you console me?' It is something giving retreats teaches: this deep need for consolation. I
read of a Russian priest remembered for saying to his spiritual children: 'How can I comfort you?' And when they and
he had finished, 'How else can I comfort you?'

Let's look for the consolations of God.

I

To turn to Scripture first. At the word 'consolation', we naturally picture something wet and warm, sweet and soft: laps
and bosoms, hugs and kisses, honey in the morning and
Horlicks in the evening. The Hebrew (*niham*) and the Greek
(*parakaleo*) are stronger than that. In Hebrew, to console is to
comfort in the sense of strengthen; it's to deliver from fear,
to revive, restore, support, help, empower. Concretely, it's
what the Lord will do to Zion fallen on hard times. 'For the
Lord will comfort Zion; he will comfort all her waste places'
(Is 51:3). It's the cessation of his anger, the gathering of the
scattered, the liberation of the deportees, the setting free of
the imprisoned, the rebuilding of the ruins, the dancing of old
and young, the cities overflowing with wealth. It's ultimately
the coming of the Messiah.

In the Greek New Testament, *parakaleo* can mean to
comfort, exhort, call to salvation, encourage, strengthen,
bless. And the Lord, himself a Paraclete, says: 'I will ask the
Father, and he will give you another Paraclete, to be with you
for ever' (Jn 14:16): an Advocate, One called in to help, the
Great Stand-by, the Spirit, who will allay the disciples' pains
of fear, trouble and bereavement. Extraordinary how one poor
human word ends up suggesting the Trinity. Consolation in
the biblical sense is the intervention of God on behalf of his
suffering people as a whole and his suffering servants individually; it is God rescuing and rebuilding, strengthening and
supporting; it is, finally, the Father sending the Son and the
Spirit. It isn't small!

So, we have consolation. It is, of course, very much an
Advent theme. 'Console my people, console them,' says your
God. 'Speak to the heart of Jerusalem and call to her that her
time of service is ended, her sin is atoned for' (Is 40:1-2, JB)
– words, in the Authorized Version, made unforgettable by
Handel. The Messiah is precisely the Comforter of Israel.
But it's also a Pentecostal theme. The Holy Spirit is the

Comforter, 'Supreme Comforter' says the Sequence, *Consolator optime*, the *best* at consoling there is. In the familiar prayer (from the Votive Mass of the Holy Spirit), we can even ask '*always* to rejoice in his consolation'. As Eastertide comes to its climax, consolation comes ever more to the fore. We hear our Lord's last discourse in the Upper Room: it's very much him consoling the saddened disciples. We hear the Acts of the Apostles, from one angle a story of how God consoled the Church amid her growing pains. We listen to the Apocalypse, consoling the embattled and persecuted: Babylon will fall and the saints will reign. Pentecost brings consolation in person, and in the heart of the Church Mary becomes the Consoler of the Afflicted.

II

'When will you console me?' He always does, as a matter of fact, but we can be too inwardly darkened to see it. Our eyes need opening. Perhaps a passage from St Aelred can help us see.

You know, beloved, that 'man born of woman lives a short time and is filled with many miseries' (Job 14:1). Yes, this life is indeed full of many, many miseries. Who could possibly count them? And it is not possible for the soul to survive among them without some consolation. The soul looks for consolation. The lovers of this world, no doubt, pursue their own consolations. 'Woe to you who are rich; you have your consolation' (Lk 6:24). So, does 'the Father of mercies and God of all consolation' leave us without any consolation? The truth is, brethren, that just as the righteous have many tribulations, so they have many consolations (cf. Pss 33:20; 93:19). We are consoled by hope of the divine promise; we are consoled by the sweetness of brotherly love; we are consoled by rich, sweet inner compunction; we are consoled by the light of heavenly contemplation; we are consoled by meditation on the divine law. And finally 'whatever was written was written for our instruction and consolation, so that by patience and the consolation of the Scriptures we might have hope' (Rom 15:4), with the first 'consolation' an addition.[2]

Here then we have a little list of the ways in which the
Father of mercies consoles the monk. It's clear here incidentally, and clear from other passages, how very conscious St
Aelred was of just how much suffering there is in human lives
and in monastic lives, especially those lived in the austerity of
primitive Cistercianism. And his pastoral heart shines out: it
isn't possible for the soul to survive without some consolation.

So St Aelred gives us this list: not exhaustive, but sugges-
tive, mentioning six ways in which God consoles. I think they
can be reduced to four: by hope, by each other, by prayer and
inner life, by the Bible.

The Consolation of Hope

'We are consoled by hope of the divine promise.' The *divine*
promise. God is our consolation. 'To commit one's hope to
God' is a precious tool of good works (*Rule* 4.41). 'It is better
to take refuge in the Lord than to trust in men' (Ps 117:8).
Even when he appears to be against us, God is on our side.
How much of our desolation comes from putting our hope
somewhere other than God! 'We are consoled by hope of the
divine *promise*.' The promise, of course, is ultimately the life
of the world to come, eternal life, heaven. Do I allow the hope
of heaven to console me? Or do I suffer from 'eschatological
amnesia'? How can the hope of God's promise really get into
my blood? Each of us has to find his own way. 'His master
said to him, "Well done, good and faithful servant ... Enter
into the joy of your master"' (Mt 25:21). Perhaps there's a
way there. One day, if by God's grace I have been good and
faithful, Christ the Lord will say to me, 'Well done.' The Son
of God incarnate will say to me, 'Well done.' He will rise
from his throne as I come forward, and say, 'Well done.' He
will be echoing his Father, and be echoed by the Holy Spirit.
The undivided Trinity will cry to me, 'Well done.' His mother
will rise and say the same in her ravishing way. The choirs of
angels in turn will sing it out in harmony. Then the crowd of
saints and friends and half-forgotten souls will break the rules
(there aren't any anyway), rush on to the pitch, and mob me
with welcome and praise ...

The Consolation of Brethren

'We are consoled by the sweetness of brotherly love.' Very Aelred, very human, very Christian. 'But God, who consoles the downcast, consoled us by the arrival of Titus' (2 Cor 7:6). Again and again St Paul was consoled by his co-workers. St Benedict, in chapter 1 of his Rule, speaks of 'the solace of many' and 'the consolation of another' which the hermit leaves behind and the cenobite enjoys (1.4–5). The 'mature and wise brothers' of chapter 27 are envisaged 'as it were secretly consol[ing] the wavering brother ... consol[ing] him lest he be swallowed up by too much sadness' (27.3). Pastoral consolation, mediated from brother to brother; often perhaps unconsciously. It may be echoed in any community, any family, any relationship. Occasionally I'm led to encourage my brethren to be present, brightly and promptly, at what we call common acts. It's precisely because these 'acts' console. The person who turns aside from them inevitably looks for consolation elsewhere, looks for 'another' than the companions God has given him. But the pain won't go. Consolation is always first and foremost to be found in the relationships, in the situations in which God has placed us, and 'the sweetness of brotherly love' is firstly and humbly, simply being and sticking together.

The Consolation of the Touches of God

'We are consoled by the richness and sweetness of inner compunction; we are consoled by heavenly contemplation.' Part of our desolation may be that there isn't much of these things in evidence. But what does St Aelred mean? Touches of God (*compunction*) and glimpses of God (*contemplation*). Surely we're not entirely bereft of them! The comfort that follows the breaking of the heart, the calm after contrition, the sense of God's guidance in a situation, an answered prayer, stirrings of the spirit, gentle confirmations of lines of thought or inner aspirations, the phrase or the psalm or the feast day or the mystery that suddenly becomes luminous. The liturgy always has power to pacify, however fraught I, or even sometimes it, may be. And like the being with our brethren, prayer deep down or at 'the fine point of the spirit' simply does let the consolation in. Even if sufferings or anguishes persist, prayer has its own discreet, subtle way of limiting or relativizing them. The spirit has its hidden veins and the Holy Spirit knows where they are. Part of me is submerged in desolation, but not all of me. Part of me can look down from above. Part of me is free just to adore. 'Richness and sweetness', says St Aelred. These words belong to the vocabulary of the Eucharist. The Blessed Sacrament is what really touches us and allows us sight of God. How desolate life would be without it!

The Consolation of Scripture

'We are consoled by meditation on the divine law ... so that [quoting Rom 15:4] through patience and the consolation of the Scriptures we might have hope.' This is what so often consoles the so often afflicted Psalmist of Psalm 118:

> I take delight in your statutes; I will not forget your word ...
> Your will is my delight; your statutes are my counsellors ... My
> soul pines away with grief; by your word raise me up ... This is
> my comfort in sorrow that your promise gives me life ... I
> remember your decrees of old and these, Lord, console me (Ps
> 118:16, 24, 28, 50, 52).

In the evening, Isaac, still desolated by the loss of his mother, went out to meditate in the field, and the Christian goes out to meditate on Scripture. 'I tell you, brothers,' St Aelred says in another sermon,

> nothing contrary can happen, nothing sad or bitter occur, which
> does not either quickly go or prove more easy to bear as soon as
> the Sacred Page explains it to us. This is the field into which the
> holy Isaac went forth to meditate, the day being now well spent,
> where Rebecca coming to meet him softened with her gentleness
> the affliction that was his. How often, my good Jesus, the day
> draws towards evening; how often to the daylight of some little
> consolation the dark night of some insupportable sadness

succeeds. All is turned to weariness; everything I see a burden. If someone speaks, I scarcely hear; if someone knocks, I am hardly aware of it. My heart is hardened like a stone. I cannot speak. My eyes are dry. What then? I go forth to meditate in the field. I open the Holy Book and write my thoughts on the tablets when suddenly your grace, good Jesus, like Rebecca running up, disperses the darkness with its light, drives away weariness, breaks my hardness. Soon tears succeed to sighs and heavenly joy comes with tears. Unfortunate are those who, when some sadness troubles them, do not go out into this field that they may be happy.[3]

So there are four 'comfort-zones' suggested by this great monk: hope of heaven, love of the brethren, sweetness in prayer, walking in the field of Scripture. It's worth repeating: it is always God who consoles. 'When cares increase in my heart, *your* consolation calms my soul' (Ps 93:19). It comes from him, 'the Father of mercies and God of all consolation'. And St Paul blesses him for it. 'When will you console me?' Perhaps one answer is: always *and* sometimes, sometimes *and* always.

III

'When will you console me?' One last thought. When we pray the psalms, we do so not just in our own name, but in the name of the Church. There are desolations other than the purely private. Simeon, nobly, longed for 'the consolation of *Israel*' (Lk 2:25), and did so at the prompting of the Holy Spirit. His heart was enlarged. For him, St Aelred's 'hope of the divine promise' meant hope of Israel's comforting. Nothing less would comfort this old man's noble heart. And I would hope we too long for the consolation of the Church and, with and through the Church, of all of suffering, desolated humanity. Was it Thoreau who said that the majority of the human race live lives of 'quiet desperation'? It seems we have to enter into the desolation of the Church (and of all humanity). And not condescendingly, from outside as it were; rather we find ourselves desolate among the desolate. Don't the terrible tales of abuse by clergy and religious desolate us? We even have to realize that we ourselves are a reason for the desolation. 'How lonely sits the city that was full of people! ... The roads to Zion mourn, for none come to the appointed feasts; all her gates are desolate, her priests groan; her maidens have been dragged away, and she herself suffers bitterly' (Lam 1:1, 4). We cry out again, in more than a private sense, 'When will you console me?' But, then, the place of desolation is precisely the place of consolation. 'It is good that one should wait quietly for the salvation of the Lord' (Lam 3:26). We wait for the word and deed of God: 'As one whom his mother comforts, so I will comfort you; you shall be comforted in Jerusalem' (Is 66:13). In Jerusalem desolation, in Jerusalem consolation. So we wait quietly, bearing the yoke. It is God who consoles, and he knows how to!

> And I heard a great voice from the throne, saying, 'Behold, the dwelling of God is with men. He will dwell with them, and they shall be his people, and God himself will be with them; he will wipe away every tear from their eyes, and death shall be no more, neither shall there be mourning nor crying nor pain any more, for the former things have passed away' (Rev 21:3-4).

And I, and we, will be consoled.

Notes

1. St Augustine, *The City of God*, XVIII, 51, 2.
2. St Aelred, *Sermo* LV, 2-3, 11.14-28, on the Feast of St Benedict (March 21).
3. St Aelred, *Sermon 27, On the Burdens of Isaiah*.

16

Scripture and Contemplation

I

In his familiar description of the four rungs of his *Ladder of Monks*, Guigo the Carthusian begins with reading and ends with contemplation. So, first a word about *lectio*, then about contemplation.

Lectio is the nourishment of contemplation. It is to the exiled spirit what a photograph of parents or spouse or children is to an exiled man. *Lectio divina*, the reflective and prayerful reading of the Bible, is much more than a pious exercise expected to deliver a private message from the Lord. It has more to do with the forming, re-forming, transforming of our whole personality. It is for the purifying of our imagination, since Scripture (so full of stories) is addressed to our imagination, our inner senses, just as the sacraments are addressed to our outer senses – and for the same reasons: God coming to us as we are so as to raise us up. It's a purification and enlargement of our memory too. As children, we learn the history of our country. As adults, we can get interested in the history of our family. As Christians, through the Bible, we are able to remember even more. The story of Israel and her great figures, of Christ and the first Christians, becomes ours. Again, reading the Bible brings our understanding and judgement into line with, union with God's. (The more we read the Bible, the more we can 'read' life.) And so the Word reaches to our heart and our will, and re-forms from within the 'body' of our life. It, too, will conform us to the paschal mystery, and so make us true contemplatives.

In the West (and not the West alone), Christians are compelled
to live in environments which are not as a rule favourable to
their faith, and often inimical to it. And we lack, not just a
wider endorsement from society, but the cultural supports and
props to our senses and imagination, the agreed outlook, the
common rituals, the all-pervading symbolism or iconography
which many of our ancestors in the Faith enjoyed. Perhaps
monasteries are now the only places where the uninhibited
expression of faith is possible, where the Sign of the Cross can
be made without self-consciousness. And this – this desert,
exile experience – is why we need, more than ever, to return
to the Bible and to enrich our liturgy. *Lectio* and liturgy will
do more than anything to keep us Christian, more, that is,
than at the merely conscious levels.

'May the sun on rising find you with a Bible in your hand,'
said Evagrius. 'I am not a monk, some of you say ... But
your mistake is in believing that the reading of the Scriptures
concerns only monks, because for you it is still more necessary since you are in the midst of the world.' So said St John
Chrysostom. 'More necessary', to counter the many counter
currents.

Scripture, said Origen, is like the *donkey* on which Christ
rides into the Jerusalem of the soul, purifying it and expelling
from it all thought of buying and selling. Or it is the *white
horse* of the Apocalypse on which he rides towards us. It (the
Old Testament anyway) is the *jars of water* at the wedding of
Cana, now turned to wine. 'Before Jesus, the scripture was
water, but after Jesus it has become wine for us.' It's the
fringe of his garment. The woman with the haemorrhage had
tried many doctors (philosophers) to no avail; then she saw
Christ and even the fringe of his garment did the trick. Scripture is the *field* where the treasure of wisdom, of Christ, is
hidden. Scripture is the *net*, woven of many thoughts, in
which we fish can be caught for God. Scripture is the '*lamp*
shining in a dark place, until the day dawns and the morning

star rises in [our] hearts' (2 Pet 1:19), and contemplation in the darkness of faith will give way to the vision face to face.

Scripture guides us into the paschal mystery and keeps us within it. It is 'the word of the cross' (1 Cor 1:18). And so . . .

II

What is contemplation? Two descriptions have helped me. First, the words of Gerontius to the Angel: 'I would have nothing but to speak with thee/For speaking's sake. I wish to hold with thee/Conscious communion';[1] and the conclusion of a discussion on happiness held by a group of men in a concentration camp: 'happiness is being with those you love'.

Contemplation (or contemplativeness) is something prior to any formal contemplative prayer, and certainly to any form of contemplative life. How contemplation unfolds in any Christian's life will depend on grace, temperament and circumstances, but surely it will be there if that life is being genuinely lived. Contemplation is *natural*. It springs naturally, under the impulse of the Holy Spirit, from faith, hope and charity. It's not primarily a matter of practices. It's a direction, an orientation, a desire, a longing, a murmur of living water within saying, 'Come to the Father'. 'I will praise you by the direction / the setting-right / the uprightness of my heart', says the Psalm (Ps 118:7, RSV). So far as he loves the Lord, the Christian will want to 'be with him', 'hold conscious communion' with him. In the Gospel of Mark's account of the constituting of the Twelve, they are appointed 'to *be with him*, and to be sent out' (Mk 13:14). The Apostles are the first contemplatives. And in the Gospel of John, in his last great prayer, the Lord extends this *being with* beyond the Twelve to all believers: 'Father, I desire that those also, whom you have given me, may *be with me* where I am, to see my glory' (Jn 17:24) – definitively in heaven, but incipiently here below, theology will say. *All* whom the Father has given to the Son are called to contemplation; the Lord has lifted up the light of his face on us all. 'And all of us,' says St Paul, 'with unveiled faces, seeing the glory of the Lord as though reflected in a mirror, are being transformed into the same image from one degree of glory to another; for this comes from the Lord, the Spirit' (2 Cor 3:18, NRSV). The whole Trinity conspires to have us contemplate.

From this too we see how, in the end, beyond all particular paths of life in the Church, contemplation is simply participation in the Passion or Passover or paschal mystery of Christ. Sharing the Passion of Christ is the fullness of love for Christ, and the fullness of love for Christ is the fullness of being with. Sharing Christ's Passion is being-with with all of one's self, just as for Christ himself his Passion was his being with the Father to the fullest degree. And this is why the martyr is the original contemplative/mystic. When we think of contemplatives or mystics, we think of hermits in caves or Carmelites in chapels. But we should think first, after Mary, Joseph and John the Baptist, after prophets and apostles, of *martyrs*. The martyrdom of martyrs is, in fact, the supreme setting of mystical experience, the full unfolding of baptismal grace. There the conformity to the suffering and risen Christ reaches a climax, and may well take the form of a *raptus*, of a being taken beyond oneself, of a suspension of the faculties as a result of divine grace, mystical experience in the strict sense.

Many of the acts of the martyrs, modern as well as ancient, testify to this. St Stephen leads. 'And gazing at him, all who sat in the council saw that his face was like the face of an angel' (Acts 6:15) – the witness is transfigured as he witnesses. ' ... full of the Holy Spirit, he gazed into heaven and saw the glory of God, and Jesus standing at the right hand of God' (7:55). In the martyr, supreme asceticism and mysticism coincide. As an almost random example from nearer our own time, there is Blessed Marcel Callo, a working-class Breton, born in 1921, who died in the concentration camp of Mauthausen on 19 March (St Joseph's day) in 1945. He was a keen member of the JOC (a Jociste) and died because of that. A French colonel with him when he died said later:

I am an old pagan. I have seen thousands of prisoners die, but I was struck by the look on the face of Marcel Callo because there was something really extraordinary about him. It was a revelation to me: the look on his face expressed the deep conviction that he was going towards total bliss. It was like an act of faith and hope in a better life. I have never seen anything like it anywhere else with any dying person (and I have seen thousands of them), nothing like what I saw in his gaze.

Here again the transfiguring joy coincides with the suffering. Not infrequently, accounts of martyrdoms include the phrase: 'it was as if he/she/they were going to a feast'. So with our own Benedictine martyrs of El Pueyo. St Thérèse, too, a martyr in another sense, seemed to see something at the very end and to be transfigured in the seeing. The point is not the experiences themselves, but what they reveal. Being a contemplative, or a mystic, means being conformed to the crucified Christ in his sacrificial love. And so the Resurrection cannot but begin to show its face.

The paschal mystery is the proper content of Christian contemplation. But it is also the 'place' from which contemplation is possible.

'Being with those you love.' Contemplative prayer is the prayer of resting in God's presence. It's an appeasing of the desire for Christ, for the Father, and in turn its strengthening. A husband at work all day may be longing for the moment when work is ended and he can go home and simply be with his wife and family. And he will not mind very much what they all do when they're together, as long as they are together. And so we should not mind too much what form our resting in God's presence takes. It may be silence. It may be listening. It may be talking something over. It may be reading in God's company. It may be repeating a formula. *Peu importe.* What is important is that the husband has those times with his wife and family if his love is not to grow cold. Again, the husband's orientation to his hearth and home, to the loves of his life, will affect the way he works away from home and relates to others. I don't mean he will be sloppy in the first or uncaring in the second. No, but there will be a relativizing, a spontaneous ascesis, a kind of involvement – in the midst of his very commitment to work and colleagues – he cannot allow himself. Contemplation is a circumcision. An exile. 'And my lament/Is cries countless, cries like dead letters sent/To dearest him that lives alas! Away.'[2]

To bring the two themes together finally, quotations from two abbots:

> To contemplate means to enter into a relationship of faith with the God of truth and life, who has revealed his face to us in Christ. That face is revealed to us on every page of the Bible. All we need to do is to *look*: open ourselves to the light and desire that it shine in us. Look with *admiration*: ecstasy in the presence of the good and the beautiful. *With a child's eyes*, that is with a clear gaze that opens on reality as after a dream, delights in it, is amazed, and sees its perpetual newness. *In silence*: the atmosphere in which the most important communication and the deepest insights occur.
>
> On the natural plane, it is the attitude of a poet; on the spiritual plane, that of a contemplative. The Bible, as Claudel said, is 'the book of admiration and contemplation', for it opens to the eyes of faith 'the poem of God's wonderful works.' These are the deeds that reveal God's holiness in act and culminate in the mystery of Christ. Standing before this awesomely beautiful picture, what can we do but contemplate?[3]

To contemplate is to encounter the Word, beyond words.[4]

Notes

1. J. H. Newman, *The Dream of Gerontius* (Family Publications, Oxford, 2001).
2. Hopkins, 'I awake and feel the Fell of Dark', from *Poems* (4th ed., 1967), ed. W. H. Gardner & N. H. MacKenzie (OUP, Oxford), p. 101.
3. Mariano Magrassi, *Praying the Bible* (Liturgical Press, Collegeville, 1998), p. 116.
4. Abbot Bernardo Olivera, *Circular Letter* 1993.

17

The Ear of the Heart

Hearing the Cry of the Poor

In the Prologue to his Rule, St Benedict talks about the 'ear of the heart', about 'bowing the ear of the heart'. In the context, it is to the teaching of the master that the ear is inclined, and through that to the Word of God. This, as we know, is the foundation of the whole Christian life. But just as love of God contains within it love of neighbour, so listening to God includes a listening to others, and a listening in particular to the cry of the poor, a listening, we can say, *with* God. Some thoughts on this . . .

In the life of St Odilo of Cluny, written shortly after Abbot Odilo's death in 1049, the story is told of a pilgrim returning from the Holy Land who was cast ashore by a storm on a desolate island where lived a hermit. From him he learned that among the rocks were places spitting fire where the souls of sinners were being purged and from which their lamentations could be heard. The hermit asserted that he had also heard the demons complaining of the efficacy of the prayers and alms of the faithful, and especially of the monks of Cluny, in rescuing their victims. On returning home the pilgrim hastened to inform the abbot and monks of Cluny of this. 'When they heard him, the brothers, their hearts running over with joy, gave thanks to God in prayer after prayer, heaping alms upon alms, working tirelessly that the dead might rest in peace.'[1] Abbot Odilo immediately set apart the second of November as a day of intercession for all the souls in Purgatory. From Cluny the custom spread to the other houses of the Cluniac order, was soon adopted in several dioceses in France, and spread thence throughout the Western Church, giving us our annual commemoration, All Souls.

That is a very medieval story, medieval in its cast; in its stretching of our powers of credence; in its crude localization of the world beyond.

What is also not only medieval but also touching, even exemplary, is the childlike response of the abbot and monks to the message. These are true Benedictines who have really interiorized the spirit of the Rule: 'As soon as anyone knocks or a poor person calls out he should respond, Thanks be to God ... and with all the gentleness of the fear of God he is to respond quickly with the fervour of love' (66.3–4). Here it is the cry of the 'poor souls' in Purgatory which reaches, not just the porter, but the whole brotherhood, and here they respond promptly with the fervour of love, with psalms and alms – notice that combination – opening the door of eternal life to these poor, posthumous sufferers.

What is striking in this quaint tale is precisely the role of the ear of the heart, of the hermit's heart first and then that of the Cluny community. Both, as it were, had their hearts' ears 'close to the ground', were able to 'pick up', with the sensitive antennae of prayer, one of the world's secret sufferings, one of the cries of the poor, in this case of the dead in process of purification. They heard with God, and so we have All Souls. Significantly enough, the next milestone in the liturgical history of that day occurred in the second decade of the twentieth century, thanks to Pius X and Benedict XV, who also, somehow, beyond the slaughter of the trenches, heard the cry of the dead. What other cries, I wonder, might we hear?

We have another, similarly imagistic story from the life of Elder Paisios of the Holy Mountain, a Greek monk who lived from 1924 to 1994. At midnight on Easter Tuesday, 1984, he saw a valley in which new wheat was growing. He stood beyond the fence and was lighting candles. On the left of the valley, however, was a barren area full of rocks. It was undergoing an earthquake and there was a constant, loud roar. Paisios became aware that the roar 'consisted of thousands of heartbreaking cries'. He couldn't work out where they came from, but he 'felt a terrible pain at the sound of them'. Then understanding came: the valley of the green wheat was the souls of the dead waiting for resurrection. The terrible place among the rocks, on the left, was for the souls of aborted infants, and it was their cries he heard. Says his biographer: 'The vision caused him so much pain but when he recovered, although he was feeling exhausted, he was unable to lie down and sleep.' Such may be the effect of the cry of pain on the listening heart. (Incidentally, the feast of All Souls was further upgraded in 1969, just when the West began to abort in earnest.) The same monk, who for all the Athonite trappings was actually a very modern man, also observed that three great sufferings – cancer, mental illness, and divorce and its effects – mark the contemporary world.

Lest I appear to be losing theological good sense, let's go back to the Bible – and its cries. 'And the Lord said, "What have you done? Listen; your brother's blood is crying out to me from the ground"' (Gen 4:10). Listen with the ear of your heart. And thanks to that story and that verse the idea of the cry of innocent blood to the Lord has entered into human history. Every form of innocent suffering, from Abel to the last of the elect, is one great cry to the Lord, asking to be heard.

'The Israelites groaned under their slavery, and cried out. Out of the slavery their cry for help rose up to God. God heard their groaning and God remembered his covenant with Abraham, Isaac and Jacob. God looked upon the Israelites, and God took notice of them' (Ex 2:23–5). It is the cry of the oppressed, and God's hearing is revealed in response: remembering, looking upon, taking notice of; in other words, acting, and – this is the threshold of the Exodus – acting redemptively. Yes, those sensitive monks knew what hearing means.

A few verses on we have another version of the same: Then the Lord said,

I have observed the misery of my people who are in Egypt; I have heard their cry on account of the taskmasters. Indeed I know their sufferings, and I have come down to deliver them from the Egyptians, and to bring them up out of that land to a good and broad land . . . The cry of the Israelites has now come to me; I have also seen how the Egyptians oppress them. So come, I will send you to Pharaoh to bring my people, the Israelites, out of Egypt (Ex 3:7-8, 9-10).

Here again what a parade of magnificent verbs! The Lord 'observes', 'hears', 'knows', 'comes down to deliver . . . and bring up' (the pattern of the Incarnation), and then 'sends'. And he sends incidentally the man, Moses, whose life as a child had been saved because a woman 'saw' his basket and 'took pity' on his 'crying'.

Because the Lord has opened his ear to the cry of oppressed Israel – the initial event of redemption – woe to Israel if she in turn oppresses! 'You shall not wrong or oppress a resident alien, for you were aliens in the land of Egypt. You shall not abuse any widow or orphan. If you do abuse them, when they cry out to me, I will surely heed their cry; my wrath will burn . . .' (Ex 22:21-4). Another, very sombre meaning of hearing. I believe St Maximilian Kolbe used to tell his fellow prisoners, 'Don't worry; these people [their captors] will be punished.'

'You shall not withhold the wages of poor and needy labourers, whether other Israelites or aliens . . . You shall pay them the wages daily before sunset, because they are poor . . . otherwise they might cry to the Lord against you, and you would incur guilt' (Deut 24:14-15). It is impossible to go through life without offending our neighbour, and prompting cries to the Lord against us. It's why, not just in the Lord's Prayer, but at the end of our lives, mutual forgiveness must have the last word.

Jeremiah, surely, was a man with an open ear: 'For I heard a cry as of a woman in labour, anguish as of one bringing forth her first child, the cry of daughter Zion gasping for breath, stretching out her hands, "Woe is me! I am fainting before killers!"' (4:31). It's the cry of suffering Jerusalem, Jerusalem besieged, sacked, destroyed, exiled. 'Arise, cry out in the night at the beginning of the watches! Pour out your heart like water before the presence of the Lord! Lift up your hands to him for the lives of your children . . . ' (Lam 2:18).

The Christ-figure on Marvin Elliot's crucifix in our cemetery has his mouth open, suggesting perhaps his final cry. 'Then Jesus gave a loud cry and breathed his last,' says the Gospel of Matthew (15:37). 'Then Jesus, crying with a loud voice, said, "Father, into your hands I commend my spirit." Having said this, he breathed his last,' says the Gospel of Luke (23:46). This is *the* cry. This is the blood of the ultimate Abel, 'crying out to me'. The Son has taken on the human condition all the way to this first and last thing, the cry. In this cry is the cry of all innocent blood, of Israel in Egypt, of widow, orphan, stranger, poor man, the oppressed worker, of sinful and suffering Jerusalem, of the persecuted righteous, of the poor man at our door, or of souls suffering in the hereafter. And 'here,' says the *Catechism* (2606), 'the Father accepts them, and, beyond all hope, answers them by raising his Son.'

Crying and hearing, it's the rhythm of the paschal mystery, the cry of the Passion and death and the hearing, 'beyond all hope', of the raising from the dead. When the monks of Cluny picked up that 'cry' of the dead and turned it into psalms and alms, so that the dead might have rest, they were living the paschal mystery.

What the world gives off is noise. A noise that tries to hide and stifle a cry. There is the noise of cities. How noisy means of transport are! How noisy radio and television. There's a noise of entertainment and sport. The noise of journalism. The noise of stock markets. The noise of preparing for war and going to war. Where is the silence to listen to the cry beneath the noise? Wasn't Bernard Nathanson's film about abortion called the *Silent Scream*? I often think of Edvard Munch's 1893 painting, 'The Scream'. There is pagan sadness, the *lacrimae rerum*. There's Christian suffering and cries in the mystical night. There's also post-Christian anguish, which has a cry all of its own, particularly desperate.

What are the cries we can hear? And how *do* we hear? It's almost a platitude to say that everything in our life is attuned to listening *to* God, from enclosure and silence on words. It's also attuned, therefore, to listening *with* God, and hearing *like* God. 'As soon as a poor man knocks or cries out ... ' Very

strange, quite unpredictable, can be the knocks at the door of
our hearts, the cries that come to our ears. When I first visited
Ghana, I was, like many a northern visitor, entranced by the
children. I also 'knew', as sometimes one does, that these
children would face me at the last judgement. 'I was in need
– of clean water, of basic medicines, of education, of opportunity, of the Faith – and you, what did you do?' There was
an abbot I knew who came within a hair's breadth of chuck-
ing it all up and going to live with the poor. He had the sense
not to do so, but one can judge a man by his temptations, and
surely this wanting, the impulse, the pull of that cry is all to
his credit. And what's the answer to the children? I came to
see it was our monastery there. What better gift for the youth
of Ghana, at this moment of transition for Africa, than a
monastery, and all the material, social, spiritual good that
goes with it? I'm grateful Providence has given us this opportunity. I'm grateful, too, for the other opportunities that have
come our way, in Lebanon, Romania, Northern Ireland – all
of them, like the hermit's island, with their craters whence
cries rise up. I hope we have listened with God and in some
sense heard like he does.

That's the 'alms', I suppose. And what about the 'psalms'?
The book of songs we call the Book of Psalms is the biblical
book which most cries to the Lord (in which, in English
versions anyway, the word 'cry' most appears). I like to think
of the cries that come to the monastery, in ourselves perhaps
or in others, being turned in the psalmody into a cry to the
Lord, and therefore, in that very act, being heard. It is our
vocation to make the mute cries audible. The chant too is part
of this. It's the noise of the world purified. The Rosary too
has its place; it links our hearts to the listening heart of Mary.
The psalms, the prayer of Mary, the life of a monk, the purified heart: these are not really very different things. They are
balm for the world.

I spoke recently with a contemplative sister who spent ten
days visiting a friend, a Missionary of Charity, working in
Albania. The work the sisters do is admirable; the conditions,
even in the capital (or especially there) are unbelievably dire.
Together, they also went up into the hill country, where there

are many residual Catholics. There in a remote farmhouse, was a family with a rather useless father, two young children, and the mother dying of cancer. The question – does at least a nurse come to see her? – was greeted with laughter. There are no nurses. And from late November until spring, it simply isn't possible to get to the place. The woman will die up there this winter, with no medication, just her sad little family around her. How does one 'hear' a cry like that? Should the sister have stayed behind? No, one goes back, hopefully with more fervour of love. One goes back with one's heart a little enlarged. And one finds life – hopefully one gives it – in the contemplative monastic life or the life that follows Christ in the world. One falls back on the old familiars of psalmody and prayer, of mystical solidarity, of love in the heart of the Church and ointment poured out. One falls back on the consoling and mysterious mathematics of grace, whereby small actions and sufferings, symbolic gestures, can be raised to a higher power. One falls back on the One in whom we hope we are. And we hope, as some other sisters once expressed it, that we're simply helping someone somewhere. At the heart of life is the paschal mystery. Many people – by pain, famine, disease, etc. – are drawn into it willy-nilly. We – willingly – allow ourselves to be drawn into it, with them and for them. And we all are in the hands and heart of God.

May we have, in our day, those ears of the heart that the compassionate monks of Cluny had!

Note

1. Quoted in Jacques Le Goff, *The Birth of Purgatory* (Scolar Press, Aldershot, 1990), p. 126.

18

The Spiritual Senses

Reflections on a Tradition

To begin with Scripture:

'Let him kiss me with the kisses of his mouth! For your love is better than wine, your anointing oils are fragrant, your name is perfume poured out; therefore the maidens love you' (1:2–3). So opens the Song of Songs. The speaker is the woman. She is pleading for and praising the love that comes to her from her man; a love that delights her senses of touch and taste and smell. In Christian tradition, needless to say, the woman is the Church, and the one whose kisses, oil and perfume she desires is Christ himself.

'We declare to you what was from the beginning, what we have heard, what we have seen with our eyes, what we have looked at and touched with our hands, concerning the Word of life' (1 Jn 1:1). So begins the First Letter of John. John is recalling the impact of the 'Word of life', the 'Word made flesh' of John's Gospel, on hearing, sight, and touch. This was an experience restricted, one might think, to the first generation of believers, to those who knew Jesus in the flesh. But he goes on: 'What we have seen and heard we proclaim also to you, so that you may have fellowship with us; and our fellowship is with the Father and with his Son Jesus Christ' (1:3). Doesn't this imply that subsequent generations of believers can, at least in some transposed way, share the original apostolic experience, and in their turn 'hear', 'see' and 'touch' their Lord?

Finally, in the Gospel of John, we hear Jesus himself: 'He who has my commandments and keeps them, he it is who loves me; and he who loves me will be loved by my Father, and I will love him and manifest myself to him' (Jn 14:21). This is a promise valid for the whole of the Church's history.

If we put these three quotations together, and read them as believers for whom the Word of God is something alive and active, we arrive at this: that Christ is still manifesting himself and this manifestation is, in some way, *sensed* by its recipients. It can be seen, heard, touched, tasted, even smelt. We come, in other words, to a mysterious possibility of perception within us, called by Tradition the 'spiritual sense' or 'senses'.

'Is it possible,' asks Sr Edith Scholl, an American Trappist,

> to describe in human language an experience of the transcendent, ineffable God, to 'express the inexpressible despite all the obstacles that lie in the way' (K. Rahner)? Mystics of all ages have made the attempt. In doing so, they have resorted to images of hearing, touching, seeing – even smelling and tasting the divine. These metaphors taken from the senses whereby we perceive material objects in the world outside us imply analogous faculties within us by which we come to perceive the immaterial, transcendent God with a direct, intuitive knowledge. These faculties came to be called the interior or spiritual senses.[1]

Christ came, said Ps.-Macarius, 'to change, transform, and renew our nature, to create anew and mingle with his divine Spirit our soul, which had been laid waste by the passions following the first sin. He came to create a new *nous*, a new *psyche*, new eyes, new ears, a new spiritual tongue, in short new men from those who believed in him.'[2]

As so often in these matters, Origen of Alexandria stands at the beginning.

> Basing himself on a few Scriptural texts (notably Prov 2:5, Heb 5:14, and some texts from the Song of Songs) Origen constructed the doctrine that there exists a 'general sense for the divine', which is subdivided into several kinds: 'a sense of sight to contemplate supernatural things such as the Cherubim and Seraphim; a sense of hearing which perceives voices that do not resound in the exterior air; a sense of taste that can savour the

bread that came down from heaven for the life of the world; a sense of smell that perceives what St Paul thus describes: we are a fragrance of Christ for God; and a sense of touch, whereby John says that he has touched the Word of life with his hands' (*Contra Celsum* I, 48). There are, therefore, 'two kinds of senses in us: the one kind is mortal, corruptible, human; the other kind is immortal, spiritual, divine' (*Peri Archon* I, 1, 9).[3]

Especially since the German Jesuit Karl Rahner devoted two serious articles to the subject in the 1930s, the spiritual senses have occasionally featured in Christian discourse on the mystical life. A generation later, the Swiss theologian Hans Urs von Balthasar made much of them in his theological aesthetic, thus bringing them into the domain of Fundamental Theology. They are the object of a useful article by Mariette Canévet in Tome XIV of the *Dictionnaire de Spiritualité*, published in 1990, but on the other hand receive no mention in the *New Catholic Encyclopedia* or the *New Dictionary of Catholic Spirituality*. The 'doctrine' concerning them – if the word is not too grand – has a long and inevitably complex history in the spiritual tradition of the Church, and research on it is still far from complete. Yet in its own way, this doctrine can be a bearer of Good News – indeed of *very* good news concerning God's presence in our lives and our capacity to rise to that and enter into it. There is something here that can help our understanding, and therefore our living, of the Christian life.

This 'something' (of which the following is simply an amateur attempt to elicit the potential) seems to flow within Tradition in two distinct streams, each of which makes its own contribution. The first appears to have as its focus that distinctively 'spiritual' element in man's make-up which provides the human possibility for a relationship with God. The second is more concerned with the possibility of a transformation precisely of our *bodily* senses. Let us try to evoke each approach in turn.

I

The starting-point is always the coming of God, the manifestation of Christ, the irruption of grace.

'Grace,' wrote the fifth-century Bishop, Diadochus of Photicé,

> is hidden in the depth of the mind from the moment of baptism, its presence being hidden even from the spiritual sense. But when anyone begins to love God with all his resolution, then by an ineffable communication through the feeling of the mind it communicates part of its benefits to the soul.[4]

Just as our experience of the physical world stimulates our bodily sense, so the awakening of grace and love in the human heart bring the spiritual sense or senses to life. A new kind of 'seeing' and 'hearing' is born:

> This is a thing which everyone ought to know, that there are eyes which are more inward than these eyes and hearing more inward than this hearing. As the eyes in a sensory way see and recognize the face of a friend or a beloved one, so the eyes of the worthy and faithful soul, being spiritually enlightened by the light of God see and recognize the true friend, the sweetest and greatly longed for bridegroom, the Lord, while the soul is shone upon by the adorable Spirit; and thus seeing with the mind the desirable and only inexpressible beauty, it is smitten with a passionate love of God, and is led into all the virtues of the Spirit, and thus possesses an unbounded, unfailing love for the Lord it longs for.[5]

Hence arises the question St Augustine answers so eloquently:

> What is it that I love when I love you? Not the beauty of any bodily thing, nor the order of seasons, nor the brightness of light that rejoices the eye, not the sweet melodies of all songs, nor the sweet fragrance of flowers and ointments and spices, not manna nor honey, not the limbs that carnal love embraces. None of these things do I love in loving my God. Yet in a sense I do love light and melody and fragrance and food and embrace when I love my God – the light and the voice and the fragrance and the food and

embrace in the soul, when that light shines upon my soul which
no place can contain, that voice sounds which no time can take
from me, I breathe that fragrance which no wind scatters, I eat
the food which is not lessened by eating, and I lie in the embrace
which satiety never comes to sunder.[67]

Hence, too, this justly famous passage:

> Late have I loved you, beauty so old and so new: late have I loved
> you. And see, you were within and I was in the external world
> and sought you there, and in my unlovely state I plunged into
> those lovely created things which you made. You were with me,
> and I was not with you. The lovely things kept me far from you,
> though if they did not have their existence in you, they had no
> existence at all. You called and cried out loud and shattered my
> deafness. You were radiant and resplendent, you put to flight my
> blindness. You were fragrant, and I drew in my breath and now
> pant after you. I tasted you, and I feel but hunger and thirst for
> you. You touched me, and I am set on fire to attain the peace
> which is yours.[7]

In such passages, which could of course be multiplied, we
ourselves sense the 'Good News' that a doctrine of the spiritual
senses is trying to convey: the Good News that Christian life is
more than a believing of certain doctrines or obedience to
certain laws. It is, at heart, an encounter with the God who
reveals himself in Christ, and an ensuing relationship, a relationship which engages us personally at the deepest level, and
which as it develops under the stimulus of the Holy Spirit
summons forth dormant potentialities in us and makes possible
an immediate, inner, experiential 'sense', a 'tasting and seeing',
even an 'embracing', of the Lord – anticipating what in the life
to come will be not simply beatific 'vision' but also beatific
'hearing' and 'smelling', 'tasting' and 'touching', all of them
ineffable. The doctrine of the spiritual senses is part of a
doctrine of prayer, and part of the vision of man that prayer
implies and elicits. Without some such doctrine, Christianity
would be reduced, and the experience of countless believers left
without explanation. The Good News is that God is closer than
we had dreamed and there is more to us than we had expected.

As our bodies are possessed of organs of sense adapted to the physical world of which we are part, so too we have one or several 'organs' capable of perceiving immaterial and divine realities. We can 'sense God'. We are close here – and Origen is explicit about this[8] – to the beatitude of the pure of heart who 'see God'. For just as the bodily senses put us in direct and normally incontrovertible contact with whatever we sense through them – we see the tree, we smell the cooking, we trip on the kerb – so in turn the doctrine of the spiritual senses suggests an analogously direct and real encounter with God, with no dilly-dallying, nothing roundabout, to it. The spiritual sense or senses function with an immediacy shared with their bodily counterparts, and work in a way other than that of the reasoning, discursive mind. The effect is direct, unarguable; it is contact, 'experience'.

So, a little paradoxically perhaps, what this first approach to the spiritual senses brings us is a fresh understanding of the human spirit, the *mind*. It brings us to the distinction between Intellect and Reason, *Nous* and *Dianoia*, *Mens* and *Ratio*. Whereas as the second term in those pairs is what enables us to conceptualize and reason and come to conclusions, the first denotes

> the highest faculty in man, through which – provided it is purified – he knows God or the inner essences or principles of created things by means of direct apprehension or spiritual perception. Unlike the ... reason, from which it must be carefully distinguished, the intellect does not function by formulating abstract concepts and then arguing on this basis to a conclusion reached through deductive reasoning, but it understands divine truth by means of immediate experience, intuition or 'simple cognition' ... The intellect dwells in the 'depths of the soul'; it constitutes the innermost aspect of the heart ... [It] is the organ of contemplation, the 'eye of the heart'.[9]

It is this new depth in us which is woken, elicited, when God 'comes' to us, when Christ 'manifests himself', when grace – the Holy Spirit – touches us; when we give ourselves seriously to Christian living.

And this depth, for many of the Fathers and mystical

writers, is identified not with five literal 'spiritual senses' (as if a copy at the level of the soul of what we find in the body), but with a unified 'intellect' or 'mind' or 'heart' (in the above meaning). This is Origen's 'general sense of the divine', which was reduced by our fallenness to a comatose condition, and now is raised from its slumbers by the touch of God. 'The loving and Holy Spirit of God teaches us that the perceptive faculty natural to our soul is single,' writes Diadochus (29). So, as regards Origen himself, 'it can be argued that the spiritual senses are not spiritual counterparts of the bodily senses, but are, rather, different figurative expressions for *nous*.'[10] The Scholastic tradition, too, says the same in its different way:

> The spiritual senses are not five permanent powers or faculties of the soul, in the manner of the bodily senses, but transient acts of the understanding and the will supernaturalized by the infused theological virtues and the gifts of the Holy Spirit. In these acts, the soul has the impression of attaining a supernatural object giving itself to the soul as if it were concretely present. Normally, this object is God himself, or the incarnate Word. This kind of spiritual sensation, this feeling of an experienced presence can take on different modalities which recall those of the various bodily senses, sight, hearing, smell, touch, taste.[11]

The inference is that the sensory language is at best analogical, often simply metaphorical.

At the same time, much suggests how natural, how justifiable, such language remains. It was not chosen arbitrarily and it would be an impoverishment to send it to the gallows. The case for it is threefold at least.

1. It is, after all, drawn from the Bible. It is, especially, a way of reading and of keeping alive in the Church the imagery of the Song of Songs, and so of linking human love to divine and vice versa. The high-point of the former can after all be described purely biologically. But who would quarrel with the Song when it speaks of gathering myrrh with spice, eating honey from the comb, drinking wine and milk, entering the aromatic garden, drinking the juice of pomegranates and pasturing the flock among the lilies? Why then should God's

lovers, when they turn to words, restrict themselves to the austerities of theological precision? Even in moments less than ecstatic, our experience of the physical world comes to us through a quintet of senses. It is far from minimalist. And the God who comes to us in Christ outdoes even the wealth of the world he made, and, in Scripture and Sacrament especially, offers himself to be 'seen', 'heard', 'touched' and more. He comes, our poor human language needing its every resource here, as light, as word, as presence, as food and drink, as fragrance. It is all too rich and varied and subtle to be put in a single, neatly labelled bottle. 'To speak in terms simply of vision or knowledge would be to give too "flat" an impression of this experience.'[12] The beneficiary of it 'senses its strength in his bones' even, says Diadochus (14). It does very much 'take on different modalities.' It is abundant and delicately differentiated all at once. It can, it's true, strike the recipient as darkness and be felt as pain (sensory experiences themselves!), but in essence and in the end it always means the delightful, delectable, delicious. 'Taste and see that the Lord is good' (Ps 33:9). And language must seek to pay its tribute to the richness of the Gift and the richness of response it arouses in us.

Origen, commenting on the Song of Songs (I, 4), articulated this memorably:

> Since Christ is a 'fountain' and 'rivers of living water flow from him', and since he is 'bread' and 'gives life', it should not seem strange that he is also 'nard' and 'gives forth fragrance', and is the 'ointment' by which those who are anointed themselves become Christ ... And perhaps ... 'in those who have their faculties trained by practice to distinguish good from evil' (cf. Heb 5:14), Christ becomes each of these things in turn, to suit the several senses of the soul. He is called the 'true light', therefore, so that souls might have eyes with which to be illuminated; and he is called 'the Word', that they might have ears with which to hear; and he is called 'bread of life', that souls might have a sense of taste ... So too he is called 'ointment' or 'nard' so that the soul's sense of smell might receive the fragrance of the Word. And so too he is called perceivable and touchable by hand, and 'the Word became flesh', so that the inner hand of the soul might

be able to make contact with the word of life. But all this is one
and the same Word of God which, in each of these, is adapted to
the movements of prayer and leaves no sense of the soul
untouched by his grace.

2. The vocabulary of 'spiritual senses' can incorporate too
another datum of Tradition: the spiritual combat, viewed as
waged between spirit and flesh. 'But I say, walk by the Spirit,
and do not gratify the desires of the flesh' (Gal 5:16). 'The
constant teaching of the tradition is that the activity of the spiritual senses is in proportion to the discipline of the physical
ones,' as Edith Scholl says.[13] Their activity is the mystical
obverse of an ascesis. It requires the mortification, or guarding, or purification of our earth-bound senses which have
become the dogsbodies of the passions and easily lead us
astray into idolatry of the created world. In Paradise before
the first sin, says Origen, the eyes of the soul were open,
those of the senses closed. When the Bible remarks that, after
eating the forbidden fruit, the eyes of both 'were opened' (Gen
2:7), the reference is to the eyes of the senses, which from
then on would impede those of the soul. The coming of the
Logos it is, Origen goes on, which restores the power of sight
to the latter.

> Therefore, the eye of the soul of any genuine Christian is awake
> and that of the senses is closed. And in proportion to the degree
> in which the superior eye is awake and the sight of the senses is
> closed, the supreme God and His Son, who is the Logos and
> Wisdom and the other titles, are comprehended and seen by each
> man.[14]

Beneath the stark, and to us exaggerated, dualism of a passage
such as this, there lies an abiding truth. It is a question of an
inner reordering: a liberation, not from the bodily senses
themselves, but from their tyranny over us, and a restoration
of the spirit's receptivity to the light of God. It is a question
of a movement from the domain of the 'flesh' to that of the
'Spirit', from a life dominated by the exterior senses to a life
in which the interior ones are in play. And to have the 'senses'
linking the two itself gives crispness to the thought. Someone

comes to a monastery, for example, and experiences the silence, almost like a shock. The physical sense of hearing is suddenly deprived of its usual noise. But why? So that, in the silence, what St Benedict calls the 'ear of the heart' can open to the Word of God.

3. There is discernment, finally, the 'nose' for what is good and what not.

As can be verified by many of Origen's references to the spiritual senses, they enable one to discern between good and evil, and are an expression of a kind of delicate spiritual sensitivity the soul learns under the influence of grace ... so that the soul no longer simply avoids breaking God's commandments, but has a feel for God's will, a kind of 'sixth sense' or insight ... 'For that soul only is perfect who has her sense of smell so pure and purged that it can catch the fragrance of the spikenard and myrrh and cypress that proceed from the Word of God, and can inhale the grace of the divine odour' (Origen, *Commentary on the Song* II, 11). The spiritual senses are a faculty which, as Balthasar puts it, 'can be developed and improved to an infinite delicacy and precision, so as to report to the soul more and more unerringly what is the will of God in every situation'.[15]

'Our physical sense of taste, when we are healthy,' writes Diadochus,

leads us to distinguish unfailingly between good food and bad, so that we want what is good. [Analogously] ... the intellect, when it has triumphed over the thoughts of the flesh, knows for certain when it is tasting the grace of the Holy Spirit ... [It] keeps fresh the memory of this taste through the energy of love, and so unerringly chooses what is best. As St. Paul says: 'This is my prayer for you, that your love may grow more and more in knowledge and in all perception, so that you choose what is best' (Phil 1:9–10).[16]

Good can be 'sensed' and tasted; evil also, smelt even. Conscience, here, would be the word for this inner sense. It may awaken first simply to an awareness of personal sin. But that is the touch of God too. And, in the domain of faith, we talk of the *sensus fidelium*, that supernatural instinct of believ-

ers, which enables them to 'sense' what is in harmony with
the Tradition that comes from the apostles, and what is not.
Again, the vocabulary of sense-perception seems appropriate.

Such, in a sketch, is one approach to the doctrine of the
spiritual senses. It is in the end a vision of the Christian life,
and a Trinitarian one: God comes, he manifests himself to us
in his incarnate Son, and by the working of the Holy Spirit we
are, in our human spirits, enabled to 'receive' him. As faith
and love progressively take their rightful place in our Christian lives, as the effects of sin are gradually overcome, as the
heart is purified, as the whole man is spiritualized, so our
'sense' of what is good is sharpened and, above all, a spiritual 'sensing' of God becomes possible. It is not that we are
literally endowed with five 'spiritual senses', but that our
heart or spirit or mind become progressively more sensitized
to the divine, and we become aware of a capacity within us
that enables us to 'see', 'hear', 'touch', 'taste', 'scent' him.
So rich – so personal too, so individual – is this encounter that
analogies drawn from our ordinary sense-experience and the
imagery of Scripture come spontaneously to hand. The Good
News here is just how real and rich life in the Spirit can be.
It is the beauty and sweetness of God.

II

The second approach also certainly begins with the coming of
God, with the reality of grace in human life. But its focus is
not on the 'spiritual senses' awakened by the Spirit, but on our
bodily senses. The thesis is that the 'spiritual senses' are
nothing other than our bodily senses transfigured from within,
and made capable of discerning the divine in the material
realm. The boundaries between the spiritual and physical in
man are porous; the spiritual is seen as in-forming the bodily
and heightening the latter's capacities.

'I do not want you to forget, brothers,' wrote Abba Isaiah
of Scetis,

that in the beginning, when Adam was created, God placed him in Paradise with healthy senses that were established according to nature. When Adam listened to the one who deceived him, all of his senses were twisted toward that which is contrary to nature, and it was then that he fell from his glory. Our Lord, however, on account of his great love, took compassion on the human race. The Word became flesh, that is to say completely human, and became in every way like us except without sin, in order that he might, through his holy body, transform that which is contrary to nature to the state that is according to nature,[17]

that is to say, the state of communion with God.

In the light of such passages, Dom Anselm Stolz (1900–1942), the German Benedictine theologian, could explain our doctrine as

> the redemption of sense-knowledge from the dulling effect consequent on original sin. Owing to the loss of original grace, sense-knowledge has to a certain extent been narrowed down to its proper object, whereas previously it played its part after its own fashion in the process of union between the spirit and God. The bliss of the spirit found an echo in it as well. In the paradisiac state the whole man rejoiced in intimate union with God. In mystical union with God we have an analogous occurrence. The spirit rejoices in intimate union with God. By means of asceticism the Holy Ghost, the efficient cause of mystical contemplation, regains control also over the other faculties of man, and they for their part are made aware of their share in mystical union with God ... [The doctrine of the spiritual senses] asserts a spiritualization, an activity of the senses under the control of the Holy Ghost, not the presence of special senses in the spirit in contrast to the senses of the animal soul. Mystical experience can also be attested externally in the life of the body.[18]

'A Monk of the Eastern Church', that is the ex-Benedictine Fr Lev Gillet (1893–1980), in his *Orthodox Spirituality*,[19] writes in the same vein, but in connection with the 'seal' (*sphragis*) of Chrismation or Confirmation:

> The negative and ascetical aspect of the *sphragis* is the closing of our senses to the things of the world, for Christ's sake. Its positive and mystical aspect, dependent no more on our effort but on

grace, is the opening of our senses to realities until then unperceived, untasted. Our natural senses are transformed into new and spiritual ones: 'Behold, I make all things new' (Rev 21:5) ... We are, by the sealing of Chrismation, admitted to a bodily (as well as spiritual) new life, to an entirely supernatural use of our natural senses.

By grace, these are purified and 'elevated', transfigured and transposed, relocated, as it were, in the spirit, and thus returned, at least inchoatively, to their healthy, paradisical state, in preparation for their ultimate beatification. Fr Lev suggests that it is especially during the illuminative stage of the developing Christian life that this process will be experienced.

Hans Urs von Balthasar, in the different context of his theological aesthetic, seems to take a similar line.

> God appears to man right in the midst of worldly reality. The centre of this act of encounter must, therefore, lie where the profane human senses, making possible the act of faith, become 'spiritual', and where faith becomes 'sensory' in order to be human, [and later, perhaps attempting a reconciliation of the two perspectives, he speaks of how, in this encounter] ... our senses, together with images and thoughts, must die with Christ and descend to the underworld in order then to rise unto the Father in an unspeakable manner which is both sensory and suprasensory.[20]

Central here is the Incarnation. God meets us – in good contemporary fashion! – where we are. The Word becomes flesh to enter into contact with beings who themselves live in the flesh, and who, as a result of sin, are to some extent immersed in the flesh. Flesh speaks to flesh, so that 'while we know God in visible form we may be, by means of this, caught up into love of the God we cannot see' (First Preface of Christmas). We have at once victimized and fallen victim to our bodies, but the Word, through the flesh he has assumed, heals them and raises them, even here and now, to a new dignity and power.

The body is not meant for immorality, but for the Lord, and the

Lord for the body ... Do you not know that your bodies are members of Christ? ... Do you not know that your body is a temple of the Holy Spirit within you, which you have from God? You are not your own; you were bought with a price. So glorify God in your body (1 Cor 6:13, 15, 19–20).

One of the attractions of this approach is that it gives a centrality in the Christian life to that public proclamation of the Word and celebration of the sacraments we call the Liturgy. There the mystery of the Lord's incarnation extends to our own times and places. There, if anywhere, our bodily senses can be purified and lifted to a new level, becoming partners in the spiritual perception of the glory of God. The Liturgy, supposing what is to be supposed, supposing that its innate beauty is allowed to shine out, is the great training-ground and also the great playing-field of the spiritual senses. And when it has done its work of eliciting them, they/we are able to see the whole of life and the whole world in a new, 'spiritual' way, and live in it accordingly. We no longer look on it in terms of our own ego, as full of things either to be grabbed or avoided. We are able to see it, to see people and events, in the light of God and the word of God in Scripture, and the human words of the Bible, perceptible to our eyes and ears, will themselves be charged with the grandeur of the Word himself, our 'spiritual senses' increasingly sensitive to the multiple 'senses of Scripture'. We will be able to see and serve in the 'little ones', the 'least of the brethren', prisoners, poor, strangers, the used and abused:

> Christ – for Christ plays in ten thousand places,
> Lovely in limbs, and lovely in eyes not his
> To the Father through the features of men's faces.[21]

This is what one patristic tradition calls the 'contemplation of created realities'. A famous instance of the ultimate transformation available along this line – and one not without its humour – was enshrined in the tale of Bishop Nonnus who looked intently at a beautiful woman of dubious morals, with no lust in his heart or his eye, but giving praise to God with tears.[22]

A central place here, therefore, surely belongs to the

Eucharist. How can communion with the life-giving flesh of the risen Christ not redound on our bodily life? How can it not at least begin its transfiguration?

In this approach too, then, there is a vision of the Christian life, but with the accent on a transformation from within of our bodily life, and so of our life in the world. The physical and human worlds can become places of epiphany, events become occasions of prayer, even the pleasures of the senses become, in C. S. Lewis' words, 'shafts of God's glory impinging on our sensibility'. And so the world, swept though it be 'with confused alarms of struggle and flight', becomes a theatre of Christian action, and the Christian himself, his senses awake, an actor in it.

Further, according to such mystics as Bl. John Ruysbroeck and St John of the Cross among others, the joy of union with God in the spirit can overflow into the bodily realm, turning the bodily senses to the interior, and allowing them to share, at their level, in this joy. Our own bodies, in all their frailty, can become temples of the glory of God.

III

'The bodily senses transfigured or an interior sense? An effect of the Incarnation or a presence of the Holy Spirit?' is how Mariette Canévet puts the question that arises once these two approaches have been distinguished.[23] There is much here for both philosophers and theologians to cut their teeth on. For our Christian living, however, an intellectually satisfactory reconciliation of the two perspectives, if it be possible, can be left aside. Each approach has its precious truth, each can help us to a deeper appreciation of the gift of God and to a fuller response to 'the upward call of God in Christ Jesus' (Phil 3:14). It is no coincidence that the pioneer of this tradition, Origen, should also be the great protagonist of the idea of the Christian life as dynamic, as a growth, as an upward movement. Often enough those who have spoken about the spiritual senses have integrated what they have to say on them into their general view of the unfolding pattern of the Christ-life in the believer. According to this tradition, a life of faith, hope and charity, based upon the Sacraments of Baptism, Confirmation and Eucharist, will flower in new sensitivities. It will have its own 'seeing, hearing, tasting, smelling, touching'. It will be exposed to the sweetness of God, *dulcedo Dei.*

> Much labour was created for every man, and a heavy yoke is upon the sons of Adam, from the day they come forth from their mother's womb till the day they return to the mother of all. Their perplexities and fear of heart – their anxious thought is the day of death ... there is anger and envy and trouble and unrest, and fear of death and fury and strife (Sir 40:1, 2, 5).

Such is indeed the lot of the sons of Adam, and the Christian is not exempt from it; indeed he may have additional reasons for feeling it. But the Good News is that even in the 'earthen vessels' we are the treasure can lodge, 'to show that the transcendent power belongs to God and not to us' (2 Cor 4:7). And part of this treasure consists in what Tradition has called the 'spiritual senses'.

As Mariette Canévet herself suggests, in the life to come, in our risen bodies, we will see at once God 'face to face' and the glorified bodily humanity of Christ seated at the Father's right hand. What is now distinction, and even opposition, 'will be experienced as one' (col. 612). On either approach, the awakening in us of the spiritual senses is an anticipation of the life of the world to come.

A postscript from St Bonaventure. For him, the recovery of the spiritual senses is part of the re-ordering of the human person that comes about through the encounter with Christ in faith, hope and love. Christ is the 'sacred principle' or hierarch

> who restores the soul to its God-conformed likeness; the more God-like the soul becomes by grace, the more clearly it sees the truth of things, that is, the more it is illumined ... Rather than restlessness and anxiety holding a grip on one's being, one's

inner life becomes more orderly and peaceful; charity is set in order [according to the Vulgate of Song of Songs 2:4] ... That is, when our feelings, thoughts, emotions (and other internal powers) are rightly ordered to God, then we start to live in a new, virtuous way that follows the example of Christ. Not only does the grace-filled interior ordering of our lives lead us to greater 'God-likeness' but our relationship to God within continues to deepen. We begin to see the truth more clearly – the truth of God and the truth of our lives in God. And the deepening of our lives in truth is, at the same time, a deepening of life in union with God, that is, with the God who reveals himself in Christ. As the soul is made hierarchical in Christ, it becomes the dwelling-place of the Trinity. It is made a daughter of the Father, a spouse of Christ, and a temple of the Holy Spirit. In union with Christ, therefore, one enters, mystically, into the life of the Trinity.[24]

Within this process of re-ordering and growth, there occurs the recovery of the spiritual senses.

The image of our soul should be clothed with the three theological virtues, by which the soul is purified, illumined and perfected and so the image is reformed and made like the heavenly Jerusalem and a part of the Church militant ... The soul, therefore, believes and hopes in Jesus Christ and loves him, who is the incarnate, uncreated and inspired Word – the way, the truth and the life. When by faith the soul believes in Christ as the uncreated Word and Splendour of the Father, it recovers its spiritual hearing and sight: its hearing to receive the words of Christ and its sight to view the splendours of that Light. When it longs in hope to receive the inspired Word, it recovers through desire and affection the spiritual sense of smell. When it embraces in love the incarnate Word, receiving delight from him and passing over into him through ecstatic love, it recovers its senses of taste and touch. Having recovered these senses, when it sees its Spouse and hears, smells, tastes and embraces him, the soul can sing the Song of Songs with the bride ... it is more a matter of affective experience than rational consideration.[25]

For St Bonaventure, 'ecstatic love' is the human being's goal, an identification with the loving Christ on the Cross, with his pass-over to the Father. And this pass-over is completed in us not by the rational mind, the discursive intellect. It belongs to the 'apex of the mind' or, better, the 'apex of the *affectus*', and consists in a tasting and, above all, a touching. For St Bonaventure, 'spiritual touch is nothing else than the act by which the soul grasps the substance of God in ecstasy.'[26]

Notes

1. Edith Scholl, 'Sensing God', *The American Benedictine Review* 47:4, Dec. 1996, p. 341.
2. Ps.-Macarius, *Homilies* 44, 1.
3. H. U. von Balthasar, *The Glory of the Lord* I (T. & T. Clark, Edinburgh, 1982), p. 366.
4. Diadochus of Photicé, *On Spiritual Knowledge*, 77.
5. Ps.-Macarius, *Homilies* 28, 5.
6. St Augustine, *Confessions* X, vi, 8, tr. F. J. Sheed (Sheed & Ward, London, 1944), p. 170.
7. Ibid., X, xxvii, 38, tr. Henry Chadwick (OUP, Oxford, 1991), p. 201.
8. Origen, *Contra Celsum* VII, 33.
9. *The Philokalia*, Vol. I (Faber, London, 1979), p. 362.
10. Andrew Louth, *The Origins of the Christian Mystical Tradition* (OUP, Oxford, 1981), p. 68.
11. P. Adnès, *Dictionnaire de Spiritualité* VI, art. 'Gout Spirituel', col. 628.
12. Louth, p. 69.
13. Scholl, p. 345.
14. Origen, VII, 39.
15. Louth, p. 69.
16. Ibid., p. 30.
17. Abba Isaiah of Scetis, *Ascetic Discourses* (Cistercian Publications, Kalamazoo, 2002), *Discourse* 2, p. 43.
18. Anselm Stolz, *The Doctrine of Spiritual Perfection* (Herder, St Louis, 1938), pp. 211–212.
19. Monk of the Eastern Church, *Orthodox Spirituality* (S.P.C.K., London, 1945), p. 68.
20. Balthasar, pp. 365, 425.
21 G. M. Hopkins, 'As kingfishers catch fire', from *Poems* (4th ed., 1967), ed. W. H. Gardner & N. H. MacKenzie (OUP, Oxford), p. 90.
22. Cf. St John Climacus, Step 15.
23. Mariette Canévet, *DS* XIV, art. 'Sens Spirituel', col. 604.
24. I. Delio, *Simply Bonaventure* (New City Press, New York, 2001), p. 108.
25. St Bonaventure, *The Soul's Journey to God*, IV, 3.
26. Karl Rahner, 'The Doctrine of the "Spiritual Senses" in the Middle Ages', in *Theological Investigations*, Vol. XVI (DLT, London, 1979), p. 126.

19

'Seek Peace and Pursue It'

Making Peace in our Communities

La Pierre-qui-Vire, 19 July 2006

'Seek peace and pursue it': such is the theme of this 'monastic day' of our *Rencontre Monastique*. The particular subject allotted me is the search for peace in our monastic life, in our monasteries. How do we, we Benedictine communities, we houses of God under the flag of *pax*, how do we seek peace, make peace, maintain peace, communicate peace? To use the precise words given me by Abbot Luc: how does a community of monks, seeking peace, build peace? I have been asked to speak from my experience as abbot. I hope also to stimulate our discussion this morning.

This conference is in three parts.

I

'In this Place I will give Peace'

Our search for peace, the building of peace does not take place in a vacuum. It has a context; more precisely, contexts. Let me begin by touching on three of them.

First of all, we are believers, and therefore the word of God is what sustains us. Allow me to take here, not our leitmotif from the psalm, but a phrase from a prophet: 'In this place I will give peace', *In loco isto dabo pacem*. So says the Lord through the prophet Haggai (2:9). This word was spoken on

17 October 520 BC, spoken in Jerusalem to a people whose
desire to rebuild the Temple, after the return from exile, was
flagging, spoken to a people who were weary. It was a word
of encouragement. 'Take courage . . . work, for I am with you
. . . The latter splendour of this house shall be greater than the
former' (2:4, 9), that is, this second Temple will have more
splendour than the first, than Solomon's, small and incomplete
though it be now. 'And in this place I will give peace' – the
famous *shalom*, total spiritual, mental and physical well-
being, individual and social. It is clear from the context that
'peace' here inclines to the material side of its meaning: prosperity, wealth. The nations who had pillaged Jerusalem in the
past and stripped the Temple will now change and bring their
treasures and splendour (v. 7), their silver and gold (v. 8) to
the footstool of the God of Israel. But this, surely, will imply
a reconciliation with God's people and the gift of themselves.
It will be peace in the fullest sense. And so indeed in this
place, the Temple in Jeru-*salem*, the Lord will give peace
(*shalom*).

The prime context of any search for peace, for a believer,
will be this prophetic promise which, for a Christian believer,
is fulfilled in Christ. 'Peace I leave with you; my peace I give
to you; not as the world gives do I give to you' (Jn 14:27).
'With the coming of the Saviour,' writes St Cyril of Alexandria in his commentary on Haggai, 'there appeared a far more
glorious temple, one that was divine . . . Therefore it is true
that the glory of this latest temple, by which you must understand the Church, will be even greater. And those who are
involved in its construction will be given Christ, the source of
peace for all men, as a reward from God our Saviour and a
gift from heaven, through whom we have access in one Spirit
to the Father.' For one seventeenth-century English philosopher, Thomas Hobbes, belligerence and war were more
'natural' to man than peace; for another, John Locke, it was
peace that came first. Empirically, the debate does not admit
of definitive solution. Ultimately, only the word of God can
assure us that peace is his purpose, and therefore first and last.
In chapter 4 of the Rule, St Benedict, imagining two monks
'discordant', calls for the making of peace before sunset

(4.73). The Latin phrase he uses is *in pacem redire*, 'to *return* to peace'. There is profound theology there. Thanks to the paschal mystery, peace is first, peace is in possession, peace awaits our return. It is, then, always and everywhere, in the context of this purpose, this gift – the peace given and to be given – that we seek peace and pursue it. It is because the peace of Christ is *given* that it can be *sought*.

'In this place I will give peace.' Thinking of the anniversary which has inspired this *rencontre*, a second aspect comes to mind. The monastic search for peace of, I suppose, all of us here, and certainly of those of my generation, has coincided with another search for peace – that in what John Paul II called 'the house of Europe'. As a child and youth I grew up in the post-war peace. Thanks to it I have never experienced war, nor serious violence. The anniversary which has inspired this meeting reminds us how much this peace was founded in initiatives, such as the Peace Crusade, which date from that decisive second half of the 1940s. As what Winston Churchill called the Iron Curtain came down, the United States offered aid to embattled Western Europe, France and Germany shook hands, the foundations of the European Union were laid. 'In this place I will give peace.' Yes, for sixty years now, in this Europe we have enjoyed a certain *shalom*, a certain peace and prosperity (a *pax americana* if we are to be honest). 1968 did not shatter it, 1989 removed, almost miraculously, that which then most threatened it. 'At the start of the twenty-first century,' a sympathetic American historian has written, 'Europe is richer, freer and more stable than at any time in its long history ... And, above all, Europe is at peace. This is not a small achievement for a continent that in its modern history has rarely known any period longer than a generation during which the scourge of war was absent.'[1] And yet, and yet ...

When I was young I was always conscious of how this peace fell between two shadows, between a memory and a fear: one, the Second World War in which my father and all my uncles had been combatants and which filled so much of their talk, the other the unthinkable thought of a Third World War, nuclear, with Western Europe as its doomed cockpit. And even if what happened in the Balkans is past (in one sense), even if there is a slow hope at work in Northern Ireland, this peace – in the light of the word of God – is always full of shadows, some of them growing darker, with most ominous of all, to my mind, the undertow of a suicidal demography. Certainly, when I was a young man in London in the winter of 1973/4, and oil prices had soared, workers were on strike, a government was collapsing, the terrorists of the time were active, and the lights were literally out in the early evening, this peace seemed shadowy indeed and made me look for another, not given by 'the world'. If I were a young man now, would I feel different? I think not.

One of the first German citizens to be invited to speak publicly in France after World War II was Romano Guardini, priest and philosopher. On 18 April 1948 he spoke to French Catholic intellectuals on our very theme, *A la Recherche de la Paix*. He argued that mankind has now experienced a new kind of war, 'absolute war', of which the essence is the destruction of man by the powers he himself has unleashed, and that this in turn asks of peace that 'it takes on a character that it did not have before'. 'Must not peace too take on an absolute character, if it wishes to rise to the height of this kind of war?' Peace, then, requires a new level of self-knowledge, self-reflection on the part of man, a qualitatively new sense of responsibility for the power he now holds in his hands. It requires a new moral stature. 'Absolute peace is the right relationship between man's power and his life.' But how can this right relationship, this true order be achieved, without a living connection with the living God, the foundation of order? There is the way. And this God is not merely an idea, but a reality, not simply the cause of the world, but personal.

God himself guides history, and the man who believes in him harmonizes himself with his holiness. It is by doing that that man will be able to curb his own power; it will be possible in this way and in no other. Thus the fate of the whole of existence hangs on the religious decision – the affirmation or denial of faith in the living God, the affirmation or denial of obedience towards Him.

What was true in 1948, what I felt in the early 1970s, is true now, however much horizons may have shifted. In this 'place' too, that is, in our time, we need the peace the Lord gives, the peace the world cannot give. The very fragility of worldly peace impels us towards it, impels us *e contrario* to seek a peace in depth. At this point, so to speak, we cross the monastery threshold.

Three times in his Rule, St Benedict calls the monastery – that distillation of the Church – the 'house of God' (31.19; 53.22; 64.5), and once, through a psalm verse, God's temple (53.14). So, here too the gift is given. My own monastery – of our Lady and St John the Baptist in the vale of St Andrew at Pluscarden, in the northeast of Scotland – was founded in 1230 by Burgundian monks (Valliscaulians or Caulites) from near here, from Val des Choux. It was vacated at the Reformation, and became one of the many picturesque monastic ruins that dot Great Britain and Ireland. After World War II, however, the medieval ruins saw life return. The monastery was re-founded from Prinknash Abbey in England. In April 1948 – the same month Guardini was giving his talk! – five monks, initially, came north, re-occupied it, recommenced the monastic life and began the work of restoration. Many other monasteries at that time were doing similar things, though, in Great Britain, we are the only monastic community to be actually inhabiting medieval buildings. And, at the time of the re-foundation, it was given this same word of Haggai as its motto: 'In this place I will give peace.' This was an expression of hope, a little grandiose perhaps, at a time of new beginning: 'the latter splendour of this house shall be greater than the former.' But it also has proved an inspired choice, even prophetic. The Lord does communicate peace in this place, that is, to those who come, even to the birds and animals too. Those who visit or stay as guests at the monastery almost invariably, almost monotonously, speak of peace as their dominant impression. The monks in choir, said a

Baptist minister recently, 'play David's harp to my Saul's soul.' Are the bones of the buried, unknown medieval monks its medium? And how deep is this experience? Does it go beyond the psycho-therapeutic? And yet, thanks to it, some abandon the thought of suicide, some return to the peace which is the Church, ecumenical relations are forged. It is moving to observe this. It is moving for an abbot too to see the Lord bringing the troubled monk, the *frater fluctuans* (27.3), back to peace. Certainly living in a house of God, under such a word of God, faced with such a constant testimony, brings the sense that there is a work of God going on, a prophecy being fulfilled, a gift available. But then there's the return to oneself, to one's heart and its *lack* of peace. Then the anguished questioning of the poet Hopkins becomes one's own:

> When will you ever, Peace, wild wood-dove, shy wings shut,
> Your round me roaming end, and under be my boughs?
> When, when, Peace, will you, Peace? I'll not play hypocrite
> to my own heart: I yield you do come sometimes; but
> That piecemeal peace is poor peace.[2]

Yes, I realize, all the un-peace of the world is in my heart, all the un-peace of sin is in my heart, while the peace of Christ in Hopkins' imagery flutters elusively around me, looking for a place to settle. It's as if the rain falls all around, but my fleece remains dry.

So a pattern repeats itself: as the un-peace of the world turns me, *e contrario*, to the peace of Christ, so does the un-peace of my heart. This too is part of the context: I am in the house of peace and yet I'm still outside it. So I am turned to prayer and to the Rule. *Da pacem, Domine!*

Let us turn this way now.

II

'The Things that make for Peace'

So we come to the building of peace in our communities. 'For peace,' as St Augustine says, 'is so great a good that even in

relation to the affairs of earth and of our mortal state no word
ever falls more gratefully upon the ear, nothing is desired with
greater longing, in fact, nothing better can be found.'[3]
According to Luke, the Lord wept over Jerusalem as he
approached it, saying, 'Would that even today you knew *the
things that make for peace*! But now they are hid from your
eyes' (19:42). Do our cities of God draw tears from the eyes
of Christ? Or are our eyes open to the things that make for
peace? Taking the Rule and experience as guide, I offer three
'things which make for peace':

- an intention of peace,
- a symbolism of peace,
- an agenda of peace.

1. An Intention of Peace

The first mention of peace we meet in the Rule is in v. 17 of
the *Prologue*: 'Seek peace and pursue it.' The Lord for his
part, you remember, has been seeking his workman, using
words from Ps 33 (34): 'Who is the man who wants life and
longs to see good days?' We have replied, I do, *Ego*. So, says
God, if you wish to have true and perpetual life, do the three
things the following verses of the psalm propose: keep your
tongue from evil and your lips from speaking deceit, in other
words choose *truth*; turn away from evil and do good, in other
words choose the *good*; and finally seek peace and pursue it,
intend *peace* (Prol. 14–17; Ps 33:12–14, RSV).

The monastic life is nothing if not intentional, that is aimed
at a goal. It is a life energized by ultimate purpose, mobilized
by the call of a final vision. It is a quest. In chapter 58, St
Benedict famously describes it as 'truly *seeking God*'. In
chapter 2 (for the abbot, but not for him alone), he quotes the
Gospel: '*Seek* first *the kingdom of God* and its righteousness.'
Here, he says '*seek peace* and pursue it.' God, the Kingdom,
peace.

If then our communities are to be places of peace, the first
need will be for each member of the community to be a seeker
after peace, knowing that the God we seek is the 'God of

peace' (1 Thess 5:23), and that the 'kingdom of God [which we seek] does not mean food and drink but righteousness and peace and joy in the Holy Spirit' (Rom 14:17). The first need is for an *intention of peace* to take root and grow in the heart and mind of the monk or nun. Here is Dorotheos of Gaza, a contemporary of St Benedict, commenting on the same verses of Ps 33:

> When a man is worthy to turn away from evil and is keen to rest with God and do good, battles with the enemy come swiftly upon him ... As he is being attacked, he does good, but with much trouble and exhaustion. But when assistance from God is generated in him and afterwards he begins to take on a certain stability in his pursuit of what is good, then he is in sight of rest, then he steps forward towards peace, then he knows from experience the struggle of war and the joy and happiness of peace; and for the rest he ardently desires it and is keen to run in pursuit of it. And finally he obtains it, so that he possesses it and builds it into himself (*Discourse* 4, 51).

First, then, an intention of peace. It may not be what is spontaneously present in our psyches. Even if our family background does not quite deserve the sociological label 'disturbed', still we *are* disturbed and, being disturbed, diffuse disturbance. The dark mystery of the *chaos*, which God overcame in the beginning but to which sin returns us, lives within us, speaks to us, summons us, and we tend towards it. Our culture, too, entertains itself continually by the presentation of un-peace, real or imaginary, and, more seriously, presents passion and conflict as the human norm. And this culture lives within us; it is not simply outside. The intention of peace, the answer to the summons of peace, to the still, small voice, will require a profound re-orientation, a conversion of mind and heart. This re-orientation will be mobilized by several realizations. Let me touch on some at least.

That, indeed, to seek God is to seek peace, that 'God is not a God of confusion but of peace' (1 Cor 14:33), that his is 'a voice that speaks of peace, peace for his people and his friends, and those who turn to him in their hearts' (Ps 84:9), that 'peace be with you' is indeed the first word of the risen Christ to his disciples (Lk 24:36; Jn 20:19). A realization, therefore, that the peace God gave in the beginning and will give in fullness at the end, can be tasted even now, is at the heart of Christian faith and hope, desirable and to be desired.

That peace is an analogous concept, rather than univocal, that it is manifold, complex, many-layered, many-sided. In one glittering paragraph of the *City of God*, St Augustine lists and defines nine kinds (XIX, 13). Our smaller minds could be content with three: peace in ourselves, peace with others, peace with God; interior, social, theological; the three sabbaths of St Aelred of Rievaulx. But in any case, to distinguish is vital. If peace is 'the tranquillity of order',[4] there is also an 'order of peace' itself, an order between the species of peace. And the peace of Christ, be it said, can be had even in Baghdad or on the Gaza Strip.

That if peace is indeed more than the absence of war, more than a balance of power between opposing forces,[5] if it is as St Augustine says 'the final fulfilment of all our goods',[6] then it is a fullness, a completion, as the Hebrew intimates; it is a *consequence* of right relationships, the effect of justice (Is 32:17) *and* of love, a '*fruit* of the Spirit' (Gal 5:22), a crown. It belongs to the evening of the day, to Compline and its *Nunc dimittis*; it is eschatological in that further sense. It will be the older monks and nuns of our communities who embody it.

That, just as Christian freedom is the effect of a redemption, so true peace is the effect of a reconciliation. It comes from Christ making peace, ending the hostility (Eph 2:15, 16) by the blood of his Cross (Col 1:20). In other words it presupposes a struggle, conflict, toil. To be a militant for peace is not an impossible paradox and Hopkins is right to talk of 'Patience exquisite / That plumes to Peace thereafter' ('Peace').

That there is always, too, the possibility of what St Benedict calls 'false peace' (4.25), a counterfeit which stops short of a necessary struggle. This is not unknown in monasteries, in the Church. A 'mutual admiration society', in the English phrase, is not true peace. 'Do not think that I have come to bring peace on earth; I have not come to bring peace, but a sword' (Mt 10:34).

That un-peace roots in sin, in egoism, self-assertion, the passions and desires which, according to St James, cause 'wars' and 'fightings' (Jas 4:1), and that the whole ascesis of the Rule, of chapters 5 to 7 especially, is a counter-offensive to these things. So Bl. John XXIII was right to link 'obedience and peace' in his motto, silence and peace too are profoundly linked (nothing so destructive of peace as bad, even simply thoughtless words), and humility is the secret door to peace.

Such considerations, I think, help ignite the intention of peace. You may wish to add others. But on fire it must be if our monasteries are to be places of peace. Without desire, there will be nothing.

Perhaps for the young monk or nun, for those 'newly come to the monastic life' (58.1), the first call of peace will be to interior peace, peace of heart. The first discovery will be of stillness, and the first lesson the need of vigilance, of the guarding of the heart and the tongue, of discernment of the thoughts, of the constant memory of God. The Eastern monastic tradition is eloquent here. It was a determining moment for me when my novice master pointed to the chapters on peace of heart in the Greco-Russian re-working of Scupoli's *Spiritual Combat*.

2. A Symbolism of Peace

The word *pax* occurs eight times in the Rule, and half of those occurrences refer not to the idea of peace, but to something very concrete, the *pax*, the sign or kiss of peace. The references are 4.25; 53.4–5; 63.4. This is what prompts me to speak of the symbolism of peace. The *intention* of peace is enveloped and sustained in our communities by a *symbolism* of peace. Our life is full of such. The French language would speak, I think, of a *symbolique* – that is, according to *Robert's Dictionary*, a 'system of symbols'. One could say, in inelegant English, a 'symbol-system'.

When St Benedict mentions the exchange of the *pax* between the brethren and the guest, he uses the phrase *et sic sibi socientur* (53.4), 'and thus they are joined, associated, united'. And so it is more widely. We connect here with the etymology of 'symbol'. There is in our life a whole symbolic system of regular, ritual, common acts, thanks to which we are 'joined, associated, united' – in peace. Certainly, being an abbot makes one sensitive to this, and to the capacity this symbolism has – in collaboration with the intention of peace – to make peace. Perhaps the contemporary mentality, so focused on the subjective, so anti-institutional, tends to underestimate this more objective dimension. Indeed, every structure, every institution in the Rule and in our life is at the service of peace. It is a question of realizing this, and respecting it.

There are, of course, many levels here.

There is, first of all, the very human – anthropological – one of ceremony or ritual. To quote Christopher Derrick, an English lay Catholic intellectual:

> The fact is that Ceremony is the friend of peace, and of civilization too. The poet Chapman was right in making that word into the name of a goddess, and in declaring her to be our prime defence against barbarism and ruin. A distinguished modern anthropologist has made very much the same point, describing ceremony or ritual as 'the most potent and prevalent of social pacifiers'. Most normal societies – ours is a very abnormal one – have been more or less aware of this, and have therefore attached a high social value to ritual, to courtesy, to ceremony; and it is interesting to note that military societies – armies – have done so outstandingly. Battle is a very unceremonious affair, but it isn't only in battle that soldiers tend to fight. Visitors to London may have witnessed the splendid ceremony known as The Changing of the Guard, outside Buckingham Palace. Its pattern stems from the fact that it involves the bringing together, into close proximity, of two separate bodies of armed men, the Old Guard and the New Guard, members of two different and therefore rival regiments. In the rough old days of this ceremony's first beginning, such a meeting was very likely indeed to end in violence which mere discipline would be unable to control ... A stronger power was therefore invoked, that of the pacifier or goddess called Ceremony: the meeting of the two Guards was highly ritualized and thus rendered peaceful, and could become the colourful tourist-attraction that it now is.[7]

Of course, the regularities of our life may, if we let them, do no more than endorse the 'institutional mentality'. But there is no inevitability to this. If lived with a living faith, they take their place among the 'things that make for peace'.

Chapters 23 to 30 – the so-called 'penal code' – and their completion in chapters 43 to 46 contain nothing if not a strategy for peace, working, especially in the process of 'satisfaction', through an array of symbols. What equivalents have we in our contemporary monasticism? How now are the wayward reconciled, how is the corporate peace re-established?

It is, though, most naturally of the Liturgy we think, of the *Opus Dei* and the Mass, without forgetting the sacrament of reconciliation. Here we have the symbolism of peace at its most eloquent. It is not for nothing that St Benedict envisages the *Pater* of Lauds and Vespers as a privileged moment of renewing the covenant of peace (13.12–13), of being *conventi*. Everything liturgical is a sign, and the community gathering and gathered so many times a day is in itself a sign of peace, of reconciliation. It is a sign of the Church, which is peace. It points to the gathering around the Lamb in heaven, final peace. And as a sign, seven times a day, it questions me: am I a member of this body? Are we 'all one in Christ' (2.20)? It challenges my anger with my brother. Am I 'lift[ing] holy hands without anger or quarrelling' (1 Tim 2:8), as St Paul bids? For the monk the sun sets seven times a day on his anger. This coming together requires, with its still small voice, a habitual readiness to be reconciled. I am reminded of Cassian's teaching on the value of cenobitic life. It unmasks the demon of anger and forces a confrontation.

And what is true of liturgy is true also, *mutatis mutandis*, of common meals, of reunions in chapter, of recreation; of all the times of gathering. Three times in chapter 42, referring to something so simple as the community gathering before Compline, that biblical/liturgical phrase *in unum* ('together') occurs. In chapter 43, referring to prayer before meals, we meet the equivalents, *simul omnes*, *sub uno*.

In these moments of togetherness in praise and eating, a door is open, a place is set, for the peace of eternity to enter and eat with us.

Supremely this is true of the Eucharist. The peace of a
community is not that simply of the like-minded, even less that
of the naturally compatible. It is not a peace such as the world
gives. It is a peace that derives from the reconciling power of
the Cross made sacramentally present in every Eucharistic
celebration. It is the peace of the Kingdom. And this peace of
Christ is communicated to us in Holy Communion. 'Because
there is one bread, we who are many are one body, for we all
partake of the one bread' (1 Cor 10:17). Eucharistic adoration
prolongs the peace of the Eucharistic celebration. After it,
I've noticed, peace reigns in the community in a new way.

The sacrament of reconciliation, too, is a sacrament that
opens the heart to peace.

Again there is so much to be said. But the essential is here:
in the regularity, the rituals and common actions of our life
there is indeed a real *symbolism of peace*. It is not effective
ex opere operato. But given the *intention of peace*, it does its
work. It makes for peace. Humanly speaking, it works at
other levels than the conscious. Divinely speaking, it is an
instrument of grace.

This gives me the excuse, I hope, to allow Julian of
Norwich, profoundest of the English mystics, a word:

> And though we, through the anger and contrariness, which is in
> us, are now in a state of tribulation, distress and grief, as our
> blindness and weakness deserve, yet through God's merciful care
> we are certainly safe so that we shall not perish. But we are not
> blessedly safe in the possession of our eternal joy until we are in
> a state of peace and love; that is to say, taking full pleasure in
> God and in all his works and in all his decrees, and loving and
> peaceful within ourselves, towards our fellow Christians and
> towards all whom God loves, as is pleasing to his love. And this
> is what God's goodness does in us.
>
> Thus I saw that God is our true peace, and he is our sure
> support when we are ourselves unpeaceful, and he is continually
> working to bring us into eternal peace. And thus when, through
> the working of mercy and grace, we are made humble and gentle,
> we are surely safe. The soul is quickly united to God when it

truly finds inner peace, for in God no anger can be found. And I saw that when we are all peaceful and loving we shall find no contrariness, nor shall we be hindered in any way by whatever contrariness is already in us.[8]

The symbolism of peace serves this continual working of God.

3. An Agenda of Peace

Motivated by a desire for peace, supported by the symbolism of peace, we are ready now for a final step, we are ready to *act*. 'Life is for action,' Newman loved to say, and our life calls us to act for peace.

Perfect peace, as St Augustine reminded his listeners repeatedly, is eschatological only. 'Yet,' he says, commenting on Ps 33, 'we do have peace in some degree here, in order that we may deserve to have it totally there.' So, 'let us be of one heart here, let us love our neighbour as ourselves. Love your brother as you love yourself, and have peace with him.'[9] Disagreements, he adds, need not of themselves destroy the unity of hearts or kill charity. The beatitude of the peacemakers is always possible. 'Kant was right,' wrote Michael Howard in *War and the Liberal Conscience*, 'that a state of peace had to be "established". What perhaps even he did not discern was that this is a task which must be tackled afresh every day of our lives';[10] and in his 1972 lectures on *The Concept of Peace* the Anglican theologian, John Macquarrie included this wise quotation: 'The universal realization of peace is certainly not an immediate possibility. But the relative and proximate increase of peace is in every moment a very realistic possibility.'[11] 'To fulfil God's commandments daily by one's deeds' is one of St Benedict's tools of good works (4.63). Yes, there is a daily *agenda*, a daily 'fulfilment' of God's words, before us, and we can make peace by means of it.

Aside from the quotation of Ps 33, three other occurrences of the word *pax* in the Rule refer to peace in the community, peace among the brethren (4.73; 34.5; 65.11). Here is the sphere of our agenda.

It is clear from the Rule and from experience that this is a corporate activity, orchestral. It calls the whole community to action, and each member of it according to his role.

For each monk, it is clear that as St Benedict expects desire for obedience to translate into 'obedience without delay' (5.1), so he expects the intention of peace to translate into 'reconciliation without delay'. He does not wish any monk to go to sleep angry, in a state of disharmony with a brother. So, he is bidden 'to return to peace with an adversary (*cum discordante*) before the setting of the sun' (4.73), to seize the twice-daily opportunity of the full Lord's Prayer (13.12–13), to prostrate immediately before the superior or senior he has angered or disturbed, so that the current of blessing may flow unimpeded between them (71.6–8).

Each brother again, in situations of injustice, is called 'to embrace patience with a quiet mind' (7.35). St Benedict does not wish our lives to be sour milk, curdled by a sense of injustice, by long resentment, by occult anger. At one level such reactions may be justified, but they do not make for peace. Shocking though it is to say, a passion for one's own, or even another's (cf. chapter 69), justice shuts more than a few monks or nuns out from the house of peace. There is need for 'a still more excellent way' (1 Cor 12:31).

For each brother, again, contentment with the material circumstances of his life (7.49), with his own need of less or of more (34.3–4), will help build peace beyond himself: 'and so all the members will be at peace' (34.5). The demon of wanting, of artificial need, is an enemy too.

But there is need too for wise administration, good government. How often, even in monasteries (!), discontent turns on matters of food, of the provision of material needs (clothing, equipment, accommodation, etc.), and matters relating to work. Correspondingly the Cellarer has a particular responsibility for peace in the community. It is after all the chapter on the Cellarer that ends with the beautiful clause: 'so that no one be perturbed or saddened in the house of God' (31.19). The good word (31.14), the punctual provision of food (31.16), the orderly execution of business (31.18), distribution to each according to need (34), the consideration of weaknesses, the providing of help to the over-stretched (35.3–4) – all these are among the things that make for peace. And they bring us to one of the central challenges in contemporary monasticism: the preservation of balance. The balance especially between prayer, reading and work, or between the demands of work and the demands of the 'family life' of the community. It is the problem of 'stress'. There is more than one aspect here. Ideally, our communities would contain three generations. In reality, in the West, they often contain only one and a half, with a majority over 65 and a minority of active middle-aged. Thus the 'work-force' is diminished without the work necessarily being so, and a few carry many. Again, the ease of communication – above all the telephone and e-mail – multiplies communication; the ease of travel multiplies travel, and both multiply work. The agenda of peace is overwhelmed by the agenda of the mundane. Again, State legislation in our European countries impinges more and more on areas of our life, requiring ever higher 'standards' and a constant, almost neurotic, accountability. This affects any building work, accountancy, employment, 'health and safety' as it is called in Great Britain, the sale of what we produce; it affects the care of elderly members, relations with children or 'vulnerable adults', hospitality. We find ourselves like buzzing flies caught in a spider's web of legal obligations. Perhaps we need a new exodus to the wilderness, perhaps it will be provided by persecution. Or perhaps we need to insist publicly on a separate recognition, on a specific institutional status. But in daily, simple terms the problem is this: we have too much work to do. How new is it? The Desert Fathers were already familiar with the figure of the monastic 'workaholic', who creates needless work to evade the essential. Our sixth-century Rule, too, gives us a glimpse of monks saddened by heavy field work (48.7). And yet we may still feel that Wordsworth's words are truer now than ever, true even in monasteries:

> The world is too much with us; late and soon,
> Getting and spending, we lay waste our powers.

And sympathize with Georges Bernanos' magnificent line:

'the whole of modern civilization is a conspiracy against the interior life.' If so, we may conclude that, as for Guardini a world of 'absolute war' was a call to seek an absolute peace, so a world of 'absolute work' is another summons to moral evolution. Fresh imagination, serious thought and brave decisions are needed. *Omnia tamen mensurate fiant*, says St Benedict in this context, 'Let everything be done in a measured way' (48.9). 'The monks of today likewise strive to *create a harmonious balance between the interior life and work*', said *Vita Consecrata* (6). If we want an immediate criterion for such measure and balance, I suggest it is *lectio divina*. If our work so diminishes this or even excludes it that we have no holy leisure for the word of God and the life of prayerful reflection, we are astray. And only from *lectio* and prayer will we draw the wisdom we need.

In this whole context, it interests me that St Benedict calls for the exchange of the *pax*, not only between the brethren, but between them and the guest, and with prayer preceding (53.4–5). The battle for peace, the resistance of 'diabolical illusions' (53.5), the work of discernment, takes place too at this interface between the monastery and the 'world'. His insistence too, in chapter 66, that a '*wise* old man', able both to receive and give (66.1) and 'always present' (66.2), be appointed to the monastery gate, also goes beyond its literal meaning.

Lastly, there is chapter 65, *On the Appointment of the Prior*, the most vivid portrayal of un-peace in the whole Rule. St Benedict then expresses his preference: 'Therefore we regard it as expedient for *the preservation of peace and charity* that the administration of his monastery depend on the will of the abbot' (65.11). The specific threat here is what is called in English history the 'over-mighty baron', the monastery official who usurps too much 'space' for himself, perhaps tyrannizing the brethren and effectively emasculating the abbot. Dare I say it in republican France, St Benedict is a monarchist! Again, we are in the sphere of prudent administration, of good government. Again, it is a matter of balance. The situation St Benedict envisages is, in general terms, real enough. *Experientia docet*! ('Experience teaches!') There is a call upon the abbot to ensure that his service of the community is among the 'things that make for peace', that 'he does not disturb the flock entrusted to him' (63.2). He too must assume his responsibilities, without exaggeration or neglect. He must be guided by justice and charity. I need not repeat the many wisdoms found in chapters 2 and 64, but if the abbot can convey, both to each and to all, something of Christ's pastoral care, of *his* justice and love, then 'the peace of Christ [will] rule' (Col 3:15) in God's house.

'And so let them approach for the *pax*,' says St Benedict in chapter 63, v. 4, *et sic accedant ad pacem*. It is a fine phrase and may be given a sense beyond the literal. By taking up the 'things that make for peace', by using the 'instruments of peace' our life offers, we too may 'approach peace'.

III

'The peace of God which passes all understanding'

'Seek peace and pursue it.' I have been trying to trace an itinerary. It begins from the starting-points of our faith, of our world, of our monastery and the heart the monastery opens up within us. It begins from the promise of the Lord: 'In this place I will give peace.' It gathers momentum through personal intention, through corporate symbols, through concrete actions; the 'things that make for peace'. But there is one further step, one more question. And as guide here I would like to take a phrase from the Apostle Paul: 'the peace of God which passes all understanding' (Phil 4:7).

'This peace of God,' comments St Thomas *in loco*, 'surpasses every created understanding *as it is considered in its very principle (secundum quod consideratur in ipso principio).*' Yes, it surpasses all understanding, even the angelic, because it is the peace *of God*.

The remaining question is this: does the monastic quest of peace mean anything outside itself? Are we trying to walk through the battlefield with a rose in our hand, or does our search for God, for his Kingdom, for peace connect with that of those who, often heroically, seek to make peace in the world? Do we, with all our weakness, have something to give? Is there a monastic contribution?

I am among those who believe that Pope Paul VI's famous words to the General Assembly of the United Nations, 'War never again! War never again!', were not fatuous. Nor were John Paul II's repeated calls to the political communities to make war a matter of past history. Such a moral evolution is certainly difficult, will always have the mystery of iniquity pitted against it, but it is not impossible. But even if this were an unfounded hope, even if all we can ever do is mitigate the effects of man's inhumanity to man, still there is, I also believe, a Christian-monastic task, a Christian-monastic contribution.

I can only make suggestions towards, not its definition, but its designation.

A first thought is this, that just as everything within the monk and the monastery is and can be part of the search for peace, so everything that flows from the monk and the monastery is and can be part of the 'monastic contribution'. As it is *ad intra*, so it is *ad extra*. It is a matter of a whole life, a whole style of life.

In Africa, this peace-making can have a medieval vividness to it. When there was trouble, including shooting, in the larger local village near our monastery in Ghana, it was to the monastery that a good thousand people fled for refuge. When the line of the civil war in Ivory Coast passed through Bouaké and the monks took refuge elsewhere, no one pillaged the monastery; it was recognized as a haven of peace. When the monks and nuns came to Koubri in 1963, the area around their monasteries was wild and uninhabited; now it is the most developed in Burkina Faso. In Europe, the colours are softer perhaps, at least currently. But the participation in the liturgy our monasteries offer, the hospitality, the listening ear, the opportunities for ecumenical and inter-faith dialogue, the literature, even our material products are and can be all at the service of the Gospel of peace. Is it not, I wonder, the role of the oblates of our monasteries to carry the peace they receive through the monastery into their life 'in the world'?

And yet we know that the essential does not lie in these things as such. It does not lie even in prayer for peace, urgent though that always is. Rather all these things, even prayer, have value because they represent, convey something beyond themselves.

A second thought could concern the making of peace in the *Church*. Our monasteries are and can be places where the tensions between the new and the old, the right and left, the centre and the periphery are overcome. I would like to think this is truest in our liturgies, with their union of the contemplative and participative. Here too the distinct ecumenical vocations of our communities become clear (cf. *Vita Consecrata* 101).

And yet we know once again that all of this is only of value if it is translating something beyond itself.

And what name can we find for that? Perhaps it is St Paul's 'peace of God *which passes all understanding*' (Phil 4:7). It is that *peace of Christ* which, in Vatican II's words, temporal peace symbolizes and from which it derives (GS 78).

The 'monastic contribution' is our being turned, in receptivity, each of us (*singulariter*) and all together (*pariter*) towards *this* peace, this peace which passes all understanding, peace 'considered in its principle', the peace of God. This is not a 'contribution' in the ordinary sense of the word.

It is revealing that the two formal Latin commentaries on Ps 33 anterior to St Benedict – those of Augustine and Cassiodorus – are both resolutely Christological and eschatological in their interpretation of v. 15. This is the monastic instinct. 'Not as the world gives do I give to you' (Jn 14:27).

Our task, to borrow words of St Augustine from another place, is to 'relate the earthly peace to the heavenly peace, which is so truly peaceful that it should be regarded as the only peace deserving the name, at least in respect of the rational creation; for this peace is the perfectly ordered and completely harmonious fellowship in the enjoyment of God and of each other in God.'[12]

Somewhere there is the candle monk and monastery can light, the Jacob's ladder we are called to set up. St Seraphim of Sarov said it in a famous sentence: 'Keep yourself at peace, and thousands around you will be saved.'

It means, in Guardini's beautiful phrase, harmonizing with the holiness of God. It means carrying in our hearts, 'feeling' in the deepest sense, all the un-peace within us, in Christianity and in the world. It means 'suffering' this lack of peace. But carrying, feeling and suffering it, not in despair or cynicism, but in hope and for all.

'In this place I will give peace' – a call to faith.
'The things that make for peace' – a call to love.
'The peace of God which passes all understanding' – a call to hope.

The end – and the beginning – of our journey, therefore, of our monastic quest for peace, can only be the *pax Trinitatis*, the peace of the Father and the Son in the unity of the Holy Spirit.

I could therefore conclude, given where and when we are (near Dijon in 2006), with the opening paragraphs of Bl. Elisabeth of the Trinity's prayer. But forgive me if I turn to a sermon of John Henry Newman – a great fighter, indeed, but a great seeker for peace, and finder of it. The sermon is entitled *Peace in Believing*, and was preached on Trinity Sunday, 1839.

> Certainly the whole economy of redemption is a series of great and continued works; but still they all tend to rest and peace, as at the first. They began out of rest, and they end in rest. They end in that eternal state out of which they began ...
>
> All God's providences, all God's dealings with us, all His judgements, mercies, warnings, deliverances, tend to peace and repose as their ultimate issue. All our troubles and pleasures here, all our anxieties, fears, doubts, difficulties, hopes, encouragements, afflictions, losses, attainments, tend this one way. After

Christmas, Easter, and Whitsuntide, comes Trinity Sunday, and the weeks that follow; and like manner, after our soul's anxious travail; after the birth of the Spirit; after trial and temptation; after sorrow and pain; after daily dyings to the world; after daily risings unto holiness; at length comes that 'rest which remaineth unto the people of God'. After the fever of life; after wearinesses and sicknesses; fightings and despondings; languor and fretfulness; struggling and failing, struggling and succeeding; after all the changes and chances of this troubled unhealthy state, at length comes death, at length the White Throne of God, at length the Beatific Vision. After restlessness comes rest, peace, joy; – our eternal portion, if we be worthy; – the sight of the Blessed Three, the Holy One ... For there is one Person of the Father, another of the Son, and another of the Holy Ghost; and such as the Father is, such is the Son, and such is the Holy Ghost; and yet there are not three Gods, nor three Lords, nor three incomprehensibles, nor three uncreated; but one God, one Lord, one uncreated, and one incomprehensible.

Notes

1. William I. Hitchcock, *The Struggle for Europe* (Profile Books, London 2003), pp. 1, 2.
2. G. M. Hopkins, 'Peace', from *Poems* (4th ed., 1967), ed. W. H. Gardner & N. H. MacKenzie (OUP, Oxford), p. 85.
3. St Augustine, *The City of God*, XIX, 11.
4. Ibid., XIX, 13.
5. Second Vatican Council, *Gaudium et Spes* 78.
6. St Augustine, *The City of God*, XIX, 11.
7. C. Derrick, *The Rule of Peace* (St. Bede's Publications, Petersham, MA, 1980), pp. 67–8.
8. Julian of Norwich, *Revelations of Divine Love*, Long Text 49.
9. St Augustine, *Exposition of Ps. 33*, II, 19.
10. Michael Howard, *War and the Liberal Conscience* (Rutgers University Press, New Jersey, 1987).
11. John Macquarrie, *The Concept of Peace*, (Harper & Row, London, 1973), p. 13.
12. St Augustine, *The City of God*, XIX, 17.

20

Requiem Homily for Fr Maurus, 1911–2005

Readings: Wisdom 3:1–9; Romans 8:31–5, 37–9;
Matthew 25:31–46 (JB)

*The souls of the virtuous are in the hands of God, no torment
shall ever touch them. In the eyes of the unwise they did appear
to die, their going looked like a disaster, their leaving us like
annihilation; but they are in peace* (Wis 3:1–3).

Isn't it amazing how Scripture fits? Here is something written
by an anonymous Jew in Alexandria not long before the time
of Christ, read here in the north of Scotland more than 2000
years later. And it fits.

Three months ago today Fr Maurus went for one of his
walks. Despite the best efforts of the police and other services
and many individuals, there is still no trace of him. It is not
the conventional idea of a happy death. It is not a classical
monk's death, surrounded by his brethren singing the *Suscipe*.
'In the eyes of the unwise, they did appear to die, their going
looked like a disaster, their leaving us like annihilation'; no
trace, no sign, worst of all, no idea of what actually happened.
But today we are listening to other voices, to faith, hope, and
love, and what they say is: 'the souls of the virtuous are in the
hands of God, no torment shall ever touch them ... they are
in peace.' Therefore, *he* is in peace.

'When the time comes for his visitation they will shine out'
(Wis 3:7). Therefore *he* will shine out. Already, in a real
sense, he is shining out. For a decade, more or less, Fr

Maurus suffered from a form of dementia, the mind dimmed by the malfunctioning brain. It is already a form of disappearance, dementia, as anyone knows who has lived with it. And now, that affliction is lifted. And now, say the other voices, 'when the time comes for his visitation they will shine out.' Fr Maurus, for nearly sixty years, was a monk, living in community. And as in family life, so in community life, it is often less the qualities than the limitations, less the spirit's treasure than the earthen vessel, that we notice. It's not for nothing that St Benedict encourages his monks 'to bear with one another's weaknesses of body and of character with the utmost patience'. Fr Maurus too had those weaknesses, which at times needed bearing, needed the patience of his brethren. 'I have a genius for irritating people,' he once said. But that affliction too is lifted. 'God has put them to the test and proved them worthy to be with him; he has tested them like gold in a furnace, and accepted them as a holocaust. When the time comes for his visitation they will shine out' (Wis 3:5–7).

It *is* a visitation of God, this strange passing of a good man, a mysterious one for all concerned, and therefore it is a shining out. All the afflictions of old age, the contrariness, any unfinished business, belong to the past, and what the Holy Spirit made of this man can now shine out. It shines out for anyone who really knew him, who had the 'Fr Maurus experience'. It shines for anyone who ever received his memorable letters and re-reads them. It has been shining for three months in the great wave of sympathy, prayer, helpfulness and memories that have come towards this community since he disappeared. It shines – *he* shines – for so many people here and elsewhere. He shines most of all, say faith, hope and the love of God, in the bosom of the Father, in the heart of Christ, in the house of heaven.

And what is it that shines out? Today we are listening to other voices and what shines out is what we heard in the Gospel.

Then the King will say to those on his right hand, 'Come, you whom my Father has blessed, take for your heritage the kingdom prepared for you since the foundation of the world. For I was hungry and you gave me food; I was thirsty and you gave me drink; I was a stranger and you made me welcome; naked and you clothed me, sick and you visited me, in prison and you came to see me.' Then the virtuous will say to him in reply, 'Lord when did we see you hungry and feed you, or thirsty and give you drink?' ... And the King will answer, 'I tell you solemnly, in so far as you did it to one of the least of these brothers, these brothers and sisters of mine, you did it to me' (Mt 25:34–40).

It is precisely this kind of goodness, of concern, this kind of mercy, this kind of love that remains the unforgettable in Fr Maurus. It is, I think, the key to his life.

It was certainly what made him write as a thirty-three-year-old to the Benedictine monastery at Prinknash Abbey, our motherhouse in Gloucestershire. Like many a thirty-three-year-old in 1945, he was not short of experience. Liverpool Irish, brought up in a poor part of the city, losing his father at eight months, raised with two elder brothers by a noble mother who kept the family by dressmaking: all that was a real enough novitiate. He had already tried to be a missionary and had broken down when still a student. He had already discovered the lay apostolate in the form of his beloved Legion of Mary. He had worked with drunks and prostitutes and down-and-outs. He had been on the dole. He had gone through World War II in the National Fire Service fighting the fires in blitzed Liverpool. And one evening, near the end of the War, he went to the cinema and was watching the Pathé News. The first films of the newly liberated Concentration Camps were being shown.

'The film,' he wrote fifty years later,

showed the prisoners coming out of the front gate. They were like skeletons, men and women in rags and tottering on their feet. Then the camera played on a figure sitting beside the gate, just staring out, eyes bulging, in rags but obviously a woman. Her head was absolutely bald and her body all twisted. The Commentator said, 'Look at this woman. Her age is eighteen! She was arrested in Brussels when she was sixteen.' She looked in her seventies. And I thought – what was I doing? There were no fires [at that moment]. I had plenty of free time and I just enjoyed life, with little thought of war ... And I said to myself. Only prayer can penetrate a camp like that. The tanks always arrive too late. And there was still the war in the Pacific to be fought. I was haunted by the need for prayer. I knew the monasteries were places of prayer. But I did not know any monastery.

Soon after, he saw a picture in a Catholic paper. 'Prinknash Abbey', it said. He applied as a lay brother and was accepted. 'So I ended up in the monastery.' And Christ was saying: 'I was an eighteen-year-old girl, I was a victim of man's inhumanity to man and ideological lunacy, and you turned to a life of prayer for me, and for all those others in the East, in the Gulags, in the Killing Fields to come.'

'So I ended up in the monastery.' 'Ended up', though, is not quite the right phrase. Thirty-four now, he still had another sixty years. Not long after simple profession, he was sent up to re-found a ruin in Moray, now our home. It was April 1948. He was the junior of the first party of five, his companions Fr Brendan, Fr Ninian, Br Andrew, Br Cuthbert. Br Maurus was the cook – 'the first cook', as he'd proudly say, 'since the Reformation'. Fortunately for the rest of us he was better at other things than cooking! He was also the first, with one other, to make solemn profession here since the Reformation (in 1950), and the first, with two others, to be ordained priest here (in 1952). He was our last link with our beginning. Now, it isn't easy to found a monastery, to start a community in a new place. It isn't as easy as it might look to do so in a ruin. It isn't easy when your motherhouse is five hundred miles away, and the command signals may be irregular and confusing. It involves physical discomfort, an immensity of work; it means building relationships with local community, neighbours, tradesmen, the professional people; it means building a community, perhaps with some very ill-fitting stones. But from the mid-fifties to the mid-eighties, this man – who once remarked that he 'hated business' – shouldered a quite unique burden. *Si monumentum requiris, circumspice* ('If you seek his monument look around you').

Of course, many others contributed, invaluably so. But nonetheless to have been responsible, as Cellarer, for the temporal administration of the monastery for twenty-eight years, to have been second-in-command for more than thirty years, to have had care of the oblates (lay associates of the community) for forty-two years, to have been Novice Master, responsible for formation, for twenty years – and all this simultaneously – is, to say the least, impressive, all the while being faithful, visibly outstandingly faithful, to prayer, and often less than completely well. 'I was haunted by the need for prayer.' The Liturgy forbids panegyrics, I know. But honour where honour is due. It was impressive. Yet is this the heart of it? Behind the work, there was the man. This energetic, self-possessed, single-minded, masterful man, sometimes severe, often hilarious, detached and so warm, rough and gruff but capable of heart-rending kindness, full of himself but never selfish, full of Christ, full of Mary, full of the Bible, full of stories, often frustrated, always content, silent and full of pithy, punchy words that went to your heart, sometimes uncannily perceptive, always with a mystery to him: unforgettable for those who had the experience. Yet is even this the heart of it?

The heart, I think, is in the Gospel. It's in what Christ is saying through the lips of so many who experienced what shone from the man, who had the 'Fr Maurus experience'. 'I was an alcoholic, and you saved my life.' 'I was drunk, and you didn't chuck me out.' 'I was a woman, my marriage in a mess, and you rescued me.' 'I was looking for the truth, and you gave me the Faith.' 'I was a young man, young woman, who didn't know what to do with my life, and you showed me.' 'I was a nun in India, and you sustained me with good counsel for half a century.' 'I'm a priest in Congo, in Tanzania, thanks to you.' 'I'm a monk at Pluscarden thanks to you.' 'I was a novice, drowning in my own murky waters, and you pulled me out.' 'I was a novice, and you showed me the path of the life-giving Rule.' 'I was a struggling Christian in the world and your letters were my lifeline.' 'I was dying and you accompanied me.' 'I was a local, and you were just kind.' 'I was fatherless; you became my father.' As many of us know, this is just a fragment. For how many was the meeting with Fr Maurus a decisive meeting, even *the* decisive meeting of their life? 'Lord, when did we see you hungry and feed you, thirsty and give you drink?' ... And the King will answer, 'I tell you solemnly, in so far as you did it to the least of these brothers of mine, you did it to me.' 'And in the time of visitation, you will shine out.' You will shine out with this love, this care, this concern, this mercy – never, be it said, a self-chosen love, but at heart a given, an obedient one, love under the sign of the Cross.

And so we come back to the mystery of his disappearance. Fr Maurus was never conventional, never did the classical thing, and he hasn't been conventional or classical in leaving this life. There's a poem of Coventry Patmore's he much loved, called *A Farewell*.

> With all my will, but much against my heart,
> We two now part.
> My very Dear,
> Our solace is, the sad road lies so clear.[1]

Fr Maurus was famous for never saying goodbye. In interviews in the parlour, he'd just stand up and go. And he once said to me, 'I hate goodbyes.' So it is. And why? Perhaps this is the message of these strange events, whatever human resolution they may have. That there need be no goodbyes, not in Christ; only adieus, only goings to God. Fr Maurus, loyal as he was, was always bigger than what he did, more than what made him. He had prayed and built this community for fifty-eight years, and it was time to go to God. And he went, his own mysterious way, 'the bitter journey to the bourne so sweet'. Why say goodbye? Dying isn't a goodbye; it's an adieu. Death is a path. Death is a going to God. That is the essential, not how or where or in what circumstances we die. And in God there are no separations; we are one. So, 'Making full circle of our banishment', as the poem ends, we will, even in faith can now, 'amazèd meet ... Seasoning the termless feast of our content / With tears of recognition never dry.' Eternity is home, eternal life the goal, say the other voices. 'As for me, in my justice I shall see your face and be filled, when I awake, with the sight of your glory' (Ps 16:15).

'For I am certain of this: neither death nor life, no angel, no prince, nothing that exists, nothing still to come, not any power or height or depth, nor any created thing, can ever come between us and the love of God made visible in Christ Jesus our Lord' (Rom 8:38-9).

May his soul and the souls of all the faithful departed through the mercy of God rest in peace. Amen.

Note

1. Coventry Patmore, 'A Farewell', in *The New Oxford Book of English Verse*, ed. Helen Gardner (OUP, Oxford, 1972), p. 706.

Epilogue

The Assumption of Our Lady

Homily 2007

We, the abbot and monks of this monastery ... dedicate and consecrate in perpetuity ourselves and all we have, every hope and desire, by solemn prayer to the ever-loving Mother of God, and we choose her as our Patroness and Advocate.

In those words, at Vespers every year on 8 December, this community commits, entrusts, dedicates, consecrates itself to Mary. In those words, we put our selves, body and soul, our present and future welfare, fully and for ever, into the hands of Mary, the mother of Jesus. Many communities, many families, many individuals do the same. Many monarchs in the past, many gatherings of bishops, many Popes have done the same, entrusting not just themselves, but their countries, or their Christian communities or even the whole world to the care of Mary. John Paul II did this frequently. It isn't simply a modern thing. St John of Damascus, a monk and Father of the Church, preaching on this feast in Jerusalem in the eighth century, brought his sermon to a climax with these words: 'O Lady, Lady I say and again Lady ... today we consecrate to you our spirit, soul and body, each of us wholly, and with psalms, hymns and spiritual songs, we honour you with all our power.'[1] At the same period, at the other end of the Mediterranean, another monk, St Ildephonsus of Toledo, was using similar language.

I mention this approach to Mary, this putting of ourselves into her hands, as a way into what we are celebrating today. It may help us gaze into heaven and see more clearly today's great sign: 'a woman adorned with the sun, standing on the moon, and with the twelve stars on her head for a crown' (Rev 12:1, JB). This is our faith: 'The immaculate Mother of God, the ever-Virgin Mary, having completed the course of her earthly life, was assumed body and soul to heavenly glory' (Pius XII). 'Body and soul' is the arresting phrase. Of us fragmented beings it has been written, 'Body, soul and spirit cry each their own cry, and go their own way, and have no pity for each other' (George Russell); of our dying it's said by Ecclesiastes, 'the dust returns to the earth as it was, and the spirit returns to God who gave it' (12:7); for us, says the funeral liturgy, if we die in grace, 'we gain an everlasting place in heaven', but 'the body of our earthly dwelling lies in death' (Mass Preface). Christ has died and Christ is risen, and Christ's risen life is in us, in us body and soul. But we all, and even the saints in heaven, have to undergo a separation of body and soul, experience a fragmentation of a kind until at his coming Christ will reintegrate everything. 'Just as all men die in Adam,' we heard, 'so all will be brought to life in Christ; but all of them in their proper order: Christ as the first-fruits and then, after the coming of Christ, those who belong to him' (1 Cor 15:22-3, JB).

Mary, though, 'having completed the course of her earthly life, was assumed body and soul to heavenly glory.' For her Christ has died, Christ has risen and Christ has already come again. In 'body and soul' – in her entirety, wholly, completely, without remainder, and finally, forever, in perpetuity – she is taken into heavenly glory. In her the end has come, and Christ has already handed the kingdom over to God the Father, and put the last of our enemies, death, under his feet. She's completely and for ever, in body and soul, handed over to the Father, conformed to her Son, energized by the Spirit. She's wholly in the presence of God, filled with his Name and his Life and his Glory. There's nothing of herself outside this, still waiting for harvest. She's completely there, all at once, *tota simul*, 'body and soul', fully known, fully knowing, fully taken, fully given, fully alive, the Name hallowed, the Kingdom come, the Will done; Easter and the Eucharist realized in her; creation at home.

'Now a great sign appeared in heaven: a woman adorned with the sun, standing on the moon, and with the twelve stars on her head for a crown.'

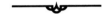

But there's more. This sign is for us. If she's present to God in such a way, so completely in Christ, so entirely the Spirit's, she will be present to us as well, the pilgrim people of God, with a fullness and a constancy all her own. Mary present body and soul to God is for that very reason present body and soul in the Church and our lives, present without remainder, undivided, with a fullness of life and energy. One could, to show this, evoke a geography, the geography of Marian places: Czestochowa, Lourdes, Fatima, Walsingham, Guadalupe and so on. Or one might evoke a history, Marian days and times in the liturgical year for example, 8 December, 1 January, 25 March, today, the season of Advent, the month of May, even Saturdays. But these Marian places and Marian moments are only as times and places of conversation in a relationship deeper than words. And the same would hold of her felt irruptions in our own lives. Mary's life, body and soul, is hidden with Christ in God, and through him, with him, in him, in the unity of the all-encompassing Spirit, wraps us round in constant, silent, hidden ways. *The Blessed Virgin compared to the Air we Breathe* was Hopkins' attempt to say this.

> She, wild web, wondrous robe,
> Mantles the guilty globe,
> Since God has let dispense
> Her prayers his providence:
> Nay, more than almoner,
> The sweet alms' self is her . . .
>   If I have understood,
> She holds high motherhood
> Towards all our ghostly good
> And plays in grace her part
> About man's beating heart,
> Laying, like air's fine flood,
> The deathdance in his blood.[2]

Or as Vatican II soberly but beautifully put it,

> Taken up to heaven, she has not lain aside this saving office [her motherhood in the order of grace] but by her manifold intercession continues to bring us the gifts of eternal salvation. By her maternal charity, she cares for the brethren of her Son, who still journey on earth surrounded by dangers and difficulties, until they are led into their blessed home. Therefore the Blessed Virgin is invoked in the Church under the titles of Advocate, Helper, Benefactress and Mediatrix (LG 62).

Words, though, fail here.

So, we come back to our beginning. How can we acknowledge all this? How respond, correspond, to what the risen Christ has given us by raising his virgin Mother, body and soul, to himself? 'My soul glorifies the Lord, and my spirit rejoices in God my Saviour' (Lk 1:46–7). Yes, by praise and thanksgiving first of all, echoing her Magnificat, calling her blessed. And yes again, by asking her prayer, for ourselves and for others, in matters small and great, now and at the hour of our death. But also, it seems, by something more. By something fuller and more constant, larger and quieter, allowing for the hidden as well as the disclosed. By, let us say (words failing again), seeking a relationship, making a gift of self in preparation for that of the world to come, lasting and total, an answer however stuttering to hers. Perhaps then we will be seeing the 'sign' of today, and find ourselves caught up in her own return to the Father.

God himself, it seems, has gone before us here. The Father entrusted his Son to the womb and the breasts and the hands and, fully and for ever, to the motherly love of Mary. That Son, on the Cross, entrusted the disciple he loved to that same mother, and 'from that hour he took her to his home' (Jn 19:27). And the Holy Spirit, in the Church, nudges Christians to entrust, to dedicate, to consecrate themselves body and soul, fully and for ever, to that same woman who is, body and soul, fully and for ever, taken up into God, and in body and soul, fully and for ever, close to us, to bring us close to her Son, our Lord Jesus Christ. Amen.

Notes

1. St John of Damascus, *Sermon I for the Dormition*, 14.
2. G. M. Hopkins, 'The Blessed Virgin compared to the Air we Breathe', from *Poems* (4th ed., 1967), ed. W. H. Gardner & N. H. MacKenzie (OUP, Oxford), pp. 94–5.

Printed in the United Kingdom by
Lightning Source UK Ltd., Milton Keynes
138495UK00001B/6/P

9 780852 446928